Special heartfelt thanks to…

Kirsten (Keesee) McKinney, my altogether lovely, devoted, and daring daughter; your overall organization and numerous, stellar contributions to this book while simultaneously planning and actually having your wedding and honeymoon were beyond remarkable! I am thankful that you keep me focused and will not let sharks deter your destiny, for God is greater!

My wonderful team, alongside the bravery of Tom Keesee whose creativity and huge heart have blessed me and made him a target for sharks, but yet he still swims on and serves passionately.

Heather Roberts, my spirited, loyal, spiritual daughter who has understood my heartbeat and faithfully served me since her early youth; great is your reward.

My husband, Gary, and children, Amy, Tim, and Polly, and grandchildren, my reasons to fight sharks.

All of these who would wrestle down a shark for me any day! And I would do the same for them (LOL)! I love and appreciate you all!

DRENDA KEESEE

SHARK
PROOF

How to Deal with Difficult People

TABLE OF CONTENTS

FOREWORD

Drenda and I have been pastors for 23 years now and business owners for 36 years. We have dealt with thousands of people, and hired and maintained hundreds of employees over the years. Unfortunately, when we started out, we had very little training or understanding of how to lead, train, and motivate people, and we were both insecure.

Although Drenda was a people person by nature, full of energy, and overflowing with ambition, she found that her own insecurities caused her to second-guess and compare herself to others. This caused her to discount the abilities she possessed. On the other hand, I was so shy and insecure when we first got married that I usually tried to avoid people altogether. Drenda has always been outgoing and a go get it done person, so I thought she could do anything when I first met her. But what I found out was that she was just as insecure as I was; we just manifested that insecurity in different ways. Amazingly, God called both of us into business and ministry, which can be defined basically as the people business! Ouch! We found out very quickly that we had a lot to learn.

Because of our sincere desire to help people, we constantly took false responsibility for everyone around us and were easily manipulated by those who wanted our position, authority, or our money. We found ourselves in so much dysfunction that we literally felt like quitting more than once. We just could not handle all of the pressure and problems that leading people required. We were bitten more than once by a shark!

As we submitted to God and allowed Him to teach us and mold us, and by not quitting, our business eventually became the number one office in the United States out of 5,000 offices. Our ministry also eventually grew to a church of thousands and hosts two international daily television broadcasts as well as conferences all over the United States and internationally. How did that happen? Well, one thing you can be sure of is that it just didn't happen on its own! There were things we had to learn and apply, especially in dealing with people. I wish I could have known many of the things we learned over the years when we first started. We would have been spared so much trouble. That is why I am so excited about Drenda's new book, *Shark Proof.*

Writing from her own experiences of dealing with the pain of people pleasing that hounded her throughout her life, she shares the lessons she learned in candid detail. Besides being a pastor, a mom who has raised our five accomplished children, and helping me oversee our businesses, she is now on a mission to help people win in life. The host of her own television show, *DRENDA*, she was honored to be asked by ABC Family to fill one of only four slots available for Christian programming on their network. Since then, her program is now seen all over the world on various networks. Drenda travels and conducts conferences in the United States and internationally with a desire to see people break free from insecurity and fear and be all that God says they can be.

In *Shark Proof*, Drenda teaches right out of her own life! She lays out what she had to learn and apply to her own life in regard to dealing with people if she was ever going to have success. A must read, *Shark Proof* will help you accelerate toward your goals and live the life of freedom that you have always dreamed of!

—Gary Keesee

BEWARE: SHARKS LURKING

In this book, I'm not talking about the kind of sharks you see on shark week. I'm talking about the kind of sharks you encounter *every* week—at work, in relationships, and even at church. I'm talking about the kind of sharks who wound you with words and accusations, take bites out of your time, rip the joy from your dreams, and leave you hopeless, injured, and floating in a sea of confusion.

If you don't deal with the sharks in your life, they'll steal your happiness. They'll use you, abuse you, and take your hard-earned money because they refuse to do what you did to succeed.

My husband and I have had to swim with sharks repeatedly in business, ministry, relationships, and friendships. As naive, immature leaders, our life during the first few years of running a business and ministry often looked like a shark feeding frenzy! At times, we agonized over our trust in the wrong people. We faced betrayals, accusations, and let people manipulate us out of money and time. We learned and kept moving forward, healing from our wounds… but many leaders don't. They give up on their passion and fall by the wayside—another victim to shark attacks.

As I've talked to leaders over the past two decades, I've discovered that Gary and I aren't the only people who learned to deal with sharks the hard, painful way. Many leaders have faced the same struggles and made the same mistakes we did. That's why I'm writing this book! I want you to know the secret to swimming with sharks too.

"Some of us learn from other people's mistakes and the rest of us have to be other people."

—Zig Ziglar

There's no escape from shark encounters. Even once you have success, sharks who envy your success and want you under their control will circle. You must learn what a shark looks like and how to deal with their games, or you will sacrifice your destiny on their attacks. God is not pleased when we allow anyone to control us or manipulate us for their profit. He doesn't get the glory when others use us to get what they want instead of seeking Him and His ways of doing things. Many people want what you have, but will they follow God and do life right to get it, or will they simply take it from you? And will you let them?

There is a tremendous freedom when we abandon the limitations that we and others have placed on us and step beyond our comfort zones. We were created to swim, but too often, we settle for second best. Or worse yet, we surrender altogether. So the question is will you be shark bait or a servant of Christ who knows how to hear direction and execute it without being trapped by distracting voices? How you handle the sharks in life will determine whether you end up a sucker, victim, enabler, or victor in the winner's circle.

PART ONE:
DARE TO SWIM

CHAPTER ONE:
GET IN THE WATER

I like to think I'm adventurous, but when the captain told me to jump in the ocean with the sharks circling our boat, I couldn't stop the blood from draining from my face. *Is this guy crazy?* We were miles from shore, deep in the Pacific Ocean. These weren't tame, aquarium sharks—not that I would have volunteered for that either—these were wild blacktip reef sharks. Let me just emphasize—*wild sharks!*

They weren't as big or scary as great whites, but even at their small size, the idea seemed crazy. Our boat wasn't sinking. I wasn't jumping into the ocean because I *had* to. Believe it or not, I had actually signed up to do this! Okay, let me tell you the full story.

Gary and I won a trip to Bora Bora through his business a couple of years back. I had always dreamed of going to Bora Bora and staying in a hut on the water. I was thrilled! When we won the trip, we also won a boat trip to swim with stingrays, reef sharks, and lemon sharks while we were there. I didn't *plan* on swimming with sharks when I said yes to get on the boat, but I'm from the south… We don't turn down *free* things—it's just not in our nature! So, when I heard they were giving us a FREE BOAT RIDE? No brainer! Sign me up!

I'll never forget the look on my husband's face when I told him what I had gotten us into. "A friend told me it's amazing," I said. "We'll just ride the boat, and if there's anything we want to do, we can do it."

After over 30 years of marriage, Gary knew better than to believe that for one second. He looked at me cautiously, knowing as soon as I saw other people having fun swimming with the sharks, I would drag us both in. What can I say? He was right! Nonetheless, I convinced him to get on the boat, and we embarked on one of the biggest adventures of our lives.

The stingrays were our first stop. They seemed fun and harmless, so we jumped in the water and had a great time. The best part was a stingray swam up to a man, and he jumped on his wife's back, screaming like a little girl. I joined suit, screaming and climbing up on Gary's back. We laughed so hard; it was a blast.

By the time we got to the sharks, I was feeling a little braver, but still unsure if I wanted to get in.

The captain of our small vessel tossed fish out to the sharks and assured me and the other couples with us that as long as the sharks had eaten, we were in no real danger.

Three words stood out. *"As long as…"*

So, they actually do eat people, I thought. *That makes me feel SO much better about climbing in the water!*

Judging by the pale expressions on everyone's faces, the other tourists on the boat were just as unsure as Gary and I were about this venture. We all waited, wondering who would make the first move.

I'll watch somebody else get in. If they don't get eaten, THEN I'll get in the water, I thought to myself, looking around to see who would be the guinea pig... or should I say shark bait?

As the intense sunshine warmed my skin, the cold, sparkling, aqua water looked like a dream. It was crystal clear—the kind of picturesque ocean you can only find in Bora Bora—but that meant you could easily see the sharks swaying back and forth as they swam near the surface. Beneath, it seemed like the ocean went for miles before it turned into a white sandy abyss.

People started diving in with their snorkel gear, and after a few moments, they seemed comfortable in the deep ocean water. My husband, inspired by a moment of bravery, followed their lead, and I looked around and realized I was left alone on the boat with all of the scared tourists. I didn't want to be grouped in with them!

There were 40 people already in the water, and I figured the sharks would get one of them before they got me. Ha! Anyway, I built up my courage and made the jump!

I didn't see large sharks in the water, only the small blacktip reef sharks swimming around me. After a few moments, I was swimming like a fish, fascinated by the creatures swimming all around me. I snorkeled around, feeling braver and braver. That's when, suddenly, an EIGHT-FOOT lemon shark swam directly beneath me. My whole body froze, and I kept my body as flat against the surface of the ocean as possible. I starting praying in my head, not batting an eyelash.

Don't show your fear. Don't move a muscle. Hold your breath.

My adrenaline was running a million miles a minute. The air caught in my throat.

That's when I noticed another massive shark appear in my peripheral vision.

Oh no, I'm surrounded! I thought.

I observed as everyone around me kept swimming normally, pointing at the sharks and even trying to touch them. My heart rate calmed, and I started to kick my legs. As I became more comfortable, a surge of excitement filled me as I observed the beautiful creatures swimming only a couple of feet below me. I felt free! It was exhilarating.

YOU CAN SWIM WITH SHARKS!

Did you know you're going to encounter sharks in your life?

The sharks I'm talking about are not the kind of sharks that swim in the water; they're the sharks that you encounter on your journey to do big things for God. They're the intimidations, the fears, the situations, and the people that will misunderstand you and that may not like you.

That's right, I said it. Not everyone is going to like you. Trust me, I figured that out the hard way!

When we know that somebody doesn't like us, most of us try to work harder to *earn* their love. We start doing more things for them and trying to perform for acceptance. I spent years as a serial people pleaser, sacrificing my needs and my dreams to the sharks that demanded them.

The toxic mind-sets of a people pleaser:

1. If I say no, you'll be mad.

2. To be loved, I have to be who you want me to be.

3. If you would just change, everything would be great.

4. I can't leave you; no one else will want me.

5. I can't ask for what I want because that's selfish.

6. I have to give up who I am so that we can be happy.

7. If you're upset, I must have done something wrong.

*Data according to Counseling Recovery

Have you ever let the obligation to say yes to people force you to say no to your needs, dreams, or priorities? I've been down that road, my friend. There's a better way!

God has a great plan for your life. He wants you to get your hopes up and to dream big, but I would be wrong not to tell you that there are going to be situations that come about which are intended by the enemy to hurt you, bother you, hinder you, and keep you back from your destiny… but the journey is worth it.

I'm so glad I got into the water, and I'm so glad I swam with those sharks. It was such an amazing experience! I felt so free!

As a mother to five brave children, I've experienced my fair share of wild adventures. Skydiving in Australia, bungee jumping in New Zealand, white water rafting in Colorado, riding trains across Europe with all five kids in tow, and driving our children in an RV from Ohio to California, just to name a few. I've also spoken to thousands, and started successful businesses, a church, and two television programs alongside my husband. Starting out as two, broke, naive young adults, these things seemed impossible—but with God, all things are possible. All of these things took courage, but bravery in relationships can be just as challenging, and even scarier!

If there's one thing I've learned after a lifetime of facing fears, it's that there's no reward without some risk. The fruit of everything Gary and I have accomplished in our lives can be traced back to one moment of bravery where we decided to jump in the water. If you are looking for a pathway to your dreams that won't require you to have courage, you'll be looking for the rest of your life.

Your dreams are on the other side of your fears! There are no shortcuts to your destiny, just one single choice: *Am I going to jump in the water?*

ARE YOU THINKING BIG ENOUGH?

Can you think of a time you had to have courage, face a fear, or stand up to a difficult situation? How did you feel after you did it?

If we don't say YES to opportunities, we limit our success... but when we have the courage to wade into the waters with God, our potential is limitless! When we face fear and overcome it, it's *empowering*.

As you go through this book, I want you to think BIG. I want you to shut down thoughts of doubt, and let your imagination run wild with your dreams. In order to jump in the water, you need to believe in yourself!

Walt Disney had a system to determine whether he was thinking big enough. After he shared his vision with his team, he'd wait to hear what they had to say. If their response was, "Sure! We can do that!" he knew he wasn't thinking big enough. He'd draw up a new plan and bring it to them. If they told him it sounded impossible, he knew that's what they were going to do.

Jesus put dreams inside of you that seem impossible in your ability. God gave you those dreams for a reason. They may *seem* impossible, but they're not through Christ! That's why Jesus encouraged us, "'*If you can?' said Jesus. 'Everything is possible for one who believes*'" (Mark 9:23, NIV).

You may feel like I did that day on the boat, eyeing the beautiful water but scared to jump in because of the sharks. You see the impossibilities, challenges, or difficult people staring you in the face. Maybe you've taken steps toward your destiny in the past, but difficult people have scared you away or tempted you to quit. It's time to let go of everything that's held you back, intimidated, or discouraged you in the past. It's time to be fearless!

If you're waiting for the perfect opportunity, the perfect training, or the perfect tools before you step out in obedience to God, you'll be waiting forever.

The one thing every successful person has in common is that they started where they WERE with what they HAD. That's all they *could* do, and that's all you can do too. The secret is they started. They jumped in. My prayer for you is that this book will teach you how to develop the courage to jump in, and once you're in, to keep swimming!

ACTION ITEMS

What are the three bravest things you have ever done?

_____

_____

_____

_____

Write down five BIG, fearless things you want to do in your life.

_____

_____

_____

_____

What dreams have you let sharks discourage or hold you back from?

_____

_____

_____

_____

Do you notice any negative patterns of people pleasing or performing for approval in yourself?

_____

_____

_____

_____

CHAPTER TWO:
LEARN AS YOU SWIM

"Most people have attained their greatest success just one step be-yond their greatest failure."

—**Napoleon Hill**

One of the hardest lessons Gary and I had to learn in business was noble failure. I *hated* the word failure... I was a straight "A" student in high school, president of my class, and voted most likely to succeed. My identity came from my accomplishments. I was terrified of failing. I thought if I did, people would retract their love from me. Because of this toxic but extremely common mind-set, I was intimidated by the dreams inside of me.

What if people didn't like me? What if I looked stupid? What if I took a risk and fell flat on my face?

There was a powerful lesson that I had to learn before I could fear-lessly pursue my dreams:

Nothing equips you for SUCCESS like NOBLE FAILURE.

I know, I know—it *seems* like an oxymoron, but it's not! Gary and I learned this lifesaving revelation at our lowest point in ministry. We had issues with our staff and with people in our church congregation, and, honestly, we were ready to throw in the towel and give up on ourselves and people.

Have you ever had a day where you were just done with people?

Want to know a secret? We experience days like that when *we* don't know how to handle the people in our lives or are letting sharks or sharklike qualities control us.

That's what happened to Gary and me. Instead of delegating to our staff the way we should have been, when a staff member brought us a problem, Gary and I took it upon ourselves to fix it. Yikes! As a leader, you can only do that so much before you're burned out and ready to move to a cabin in the woods away from people.

In addition to carrying too much responsibility in the ministry, we were allowing sharks in our lives to discourage and manipulate us. We were constantly jumping through hoops for people we *thought* had our best interests at heart, only to find ourselves disappointed over and over again by betrayal.

After years of these toxic patterns, I had never seen Gary so discouraged and worn down. One day, he came to me with tears in his eyes…

"I wrote my resignation letter today," he said, trying to fight back the crushing disappointment in his voice.

My heart sank.

I knew the situation was dire. We were on the brink of surrendering everything God had called us to do under the weight of hopelessness…

Have you ever felt the same way?

I couldn't help but ask myself: *Why? If God had called us to do ministry, why was it so hard? Why were we waking up with dread and heaviness instead of the excitement and vision we used to have?*

We were encountering the same problem many, many leaders face. We didn't know how to deal with sharks. We wanted to help people, but because we gave so much of an allowance to negative people in our lives, we lost sight of the big picture. We wasted our time on the people who couldn't be pleased, and we felt like we had failed. We felt like if we were better leaders, we wouldn't be dealing with issues. The blow was devastating.

I have seen too many business leaders, dreamers, and spiritual visionaries surrender their God-given assignments because they didn't have the knowledge we learned—the principles that equipped us to stop *surviving* around sharks and start *thriving* around them.

Let me tell you something that would have saved me a lot of heartache had I known it sooner: Sharks don't eat fish because of anything the fish do. They don't eat fish because those fish aren't good enough fish, or because those fish aren't nice enough to the sharks. **Sharks eat fish because they're SHARKS!**

If you always take false responsibility for the people who wrong you or don't like you, you will be bound by a spirit of people pleasing and, ultimately, miss your destiny! And that's the mistake Gary and I were about to make. Gary had his resignation letter written, and we were about to throw in the towel and retreat to somewhere nobody could ever hurt us again (spoiler alert: no such place exists). We were about to make a BIG mistake… We prayed for the wisdom to deal with our situation and the encouragement to keep going.

That's when God brought an incredible mentor into our lives, Dr.

Dean Radtke, and he began to encourage us and teach us how to delegate and structure our staff to alleviate some of the pressure on us. It was the breath of fresh air we needed to keep going!

Dr. Radtke taught us many leadership principles that radically changed our lives, but one of the most important principles we needed to understand as leaders was the concept of *noble failure*.

FAILURE ISN'T A FOUR-LETTER WORD.

Successful people are well acquainted with failure. For many, it was the training ground that led them to a big promotion! The secret is great leaders don't allow failure to *REDEFINE* their purpose—they use failure to *REFINE* their purpose.

Whether you fail or succeed at something *doesn't* alter the identity or purpose God placed in you. When you realize that, you don't have to look at failure through hurt, fear, or offense. Every successful person has failed before! Here are just a few:

- Walt Disney was fired from his job as a newspaper editor for lacking imagination and any original ideas.

- Michael Jordan was cut from his high school basketball team.

- Albert Einstein wasn't able to speak until he was four years old, and his teachers said he would never amount to much.

- Thomas Edison was told by his teachers he was too stupid to learn anything.

Failure doesn't mean you missed your purpose. Failure isn't the daunting, taboo word we often make it out to be. Albert Einstein once said, "Anyone who has never made a mistake has never tried anything new."

He was right! Here's the kicker. When we were children, we were actually encouraged to fail every day. You don't remember that? Maybe that's because it was given a different name. Can you guess what that was?

We called it PRACTICE! Practice is failing at something again and again until we start to fail at it less, and, eventually, don't fail at it at all.

So why, when we're adults, do we begin to look at noble failure as the enemy of our dreams instead of the pathway to our promotion?

Maybe it's because our failures become more visible the older we get. We think people expect us to have it all together, or we think our failure will disqualify us from our destinies. Perhaps our failures confirm the insecurities we have in ourselves, or, out of pride, we want to make people *think* we have it all together. I don't know why failure becomes this looming "F" word as we get older, but I do know this: **If we are unwilling to risk failure, we must be willing to sacrifice greatness.**

"I have not failed. I've just found 10,000 ways that won't work."

—Thomas A. Edison

Noble failure is simply when we do our best, try something new, and it doesn't work out the way we hoped. It's good intentions with a bad outcome. We can learn from noble failure when we dust ourselves off and move forward wiser and better equipped for success!

Giving up on God's assignment on your life because of naysayers, manipulators, fear, or setbacks is the biggest mistake we can make. Taking false responsibility for others' decisions sets you up for shark attacks. You have to learn how to deal with difficult situations and difficult people! They are never going away!

You live in shark-infested waters. You can either be afraid and intimidated or you can learn to deal with them. Whether you like it or not, there are sharks out there. There's no such thing as *safe* water—but you can be safe with God's help!

Luke 10:1-3 (ESV) tell us, *"After this the Lord appointed seventy-two others and sent them on ahead of him, two by two... And he said to them, 'The harvest is plentiful, but the laborers are few. Therefore pray earnestly to the Lord of the harvest to send out laborers into his harvest. Go your way; behold, I am sending you out as **lambs in the midst of wolves.'"***

 You must acknowledge and expect that:

- There are those around you who are not for you.
- There are people who will not like you.
- There are people who don't like your personality.

No matter what you do or how you do it, it's unreasonable to think you can please everyone or that you should try to. Just remember, to the pure all things are pure. Many times people interpret others' actions based on their personal motives, past mistakes, fears, or insecurities.

Romans 12:18 (NIV) says, *"If it is possible,* **as far as it depends on you,** *live at peace with everyone."* Pay attention to the middle of this Scripture: *"As far as it depends on* **you.**" Peace in every relationship is not always within your power. People have responsibility too. Do as much as you can to live at peace with everyone, but you can't live in a state of people pleasing and intimidation. You have to keep swimming!

If you get out of the boat, you're going to have to learn how to swim. You're going to have to learn to adapt, think new thoughts, and learn new skill sets. You're going to have to change, and that's what God wants! God wants us to get out of the boat, get into the water, and learn as we go. When you jump in the water, you're bound to miss some things. You might make some mistakes. The good news is if you keep a right heart, you can learn from the situations and move forward better equipped for success!

"Success is stumbling from failure to failure with no loss of enthusiasm."

—**Winston Churchill**

ACTION ITEMS

Today, try something new! Go to a new restaurant, try a new hobby, or go somewhere you've never been before. Here's a crazy idea: Why don't you go on an overnight road trip this weekend to somewhere you've never been?

You might be thinking, *"Drenda, I can't do that!"* Why not? What if you did? Sure, you might have to rearrange some things in your schedule, but wouldn't it be worth trying?

There's a whole world out there waiting for you to say yes to new possibilities! You can find a million excuses to live a safe, boring life, but that's not why you're here. You're here because you want to swim with sharks. The options are endless. Be bold and get out of your comfort zone this week!

Write about something new you tried this week. How did it go? How did you feel afterward?

_____

_____

_____

_____

_____

_____

CHAPTER THREE:
DON'T BUILD ON A SANDBAR

This is one of the most powerful principles I've learned about sharks: they like to make people doubt themselves. They tempt us to take shortcuts. They encourage us to *settle* for less than God promised. I want to encourage you, don't settle—build the dream God has given you!

Jim Carrey, one of the most successful actors and comedians of our day, learned a powerful lesson from his father. This is what he had to say about it:

> My father could have been a great comedian, but he didn't believe that was possible for him, and so he made a conservative choice. Instead, he got a safe job as an accountant, and when I was 12 years old, he was let go from that safe job, and our family had to do whatever we could to survive.

> I learned many great lessons from my father, not the least of which was that **you can fail at what you don't want, so you might as well take a chance on doing what you love.**

Jim Carrey made a great point! You risk failure no matter what you do, so why not do what you love? You can always find a reason to hesitate, to quit, or to delay jumping headfirst into your dreams, but you'll never step into the call on your life until you do.

Vera Wang didn't design her first wedding dress until the age of 40.

Julia Child published her first cookbook at age 39, and didn't debut on television until the age of 51.

Helen Keller, completely blind and deaf before age two, learned to read and write. Against all odds, she received her bachelor's degree and went on to write books.

At age 45, **Henry Ford** created the famous Model T car.

Anna Mary Robertson Moses, also known as Grandma Moses, started her painting career when she was 78 years old. Now, her paintings sell for millions.

One of my favorite stories belongs to singer Susan Boyle. She was 48 years old when she auditioned for *Britain's Got Talent*, and as she walked onto the stage with a cheeky grin on her face, the whole room quickly set their expectations for her to fail. She didn't come packaged as your typical "superstar." When Susan told the judges her age, they passed looks between each other. As Susan told Simon Cowell she wanted to be a professional singer as good as Elliot Paige, the camera showed audience members laughing in disbelief.

Then, Susan began to sing, and nothing short of bewilderment seized the entire audience as her voice soared. People began to stand and cheer, and even cry. Susan Boyle went on to break records with one of Britain's fastest-selling debut albums of all time. Susan said, "*There are enough people in the world who are going to write you off. You don't need to do that to yourself.*" Wise words!

God has put incredible gifts and talents in you. Even if people have overlooked them and discounted your ability, you've failed in the past, or circumstances have choked out your dreams, today is a new day. No matter what has happened, don't give up!

"When everything seems to be going against you, remember that an airplane takes off against the wind, not with it."

—Henry Ford

Stay the Course

If we live in a place of hurt, how can we be effective in our own lives or in impacting others?

Hurt feelings destroy so many relationships. Not only that, but they can take us off course from our destinies if we let them. We all do and say things that unintentionally hurt people at times. Most of these slights and misunderstandings are just that— misunderstandings! No matter what others do to us, we have to make the choice to walk in integrity, forgiveness, and to stay the course. You can't build a strong house on a crooked foundation.

Matthew 7:24-27 (NIV) say:

> *Therefore everyone who hears these words of mine and puts them into practice is like a wise man who built his house on the rock. The rain came down, the streams rose, and the winds blew and beat against that house; yet it did not fall, because it had its foundation on the rock. But everyone who hears these words of mine and does not put them into practice is like a foolish man who built his house on sand. The rain came down, the streams rose, and the winds blew and beat against that house, and it fell with a great crash.*

Don't build your life on a sandbar!

It's sad to see how mean-spirited and intolerant people can be while demanding tolerance for "their" views. While we can't change this in others, we can work on our relationships and especially ourselves.

After years of working with people and observing my own shortcomings, I've come to the conclusion that our egos, or may I say our *pride*, often gets in the way of relationships. We're all looking for others to make us feel special, valued, and even exceptional; and when others fail to do what we need, we get our feelings hurt. We retreat, sulk, and even punish the other person with our withdrawal! I've watched friendships be destroyed, marriages broken, families devastated, businesses fail, and, worse, God's Kingdom hindered, all because of pride.

Yikes!

Social media has created an opportunity for people to take their hurts to a whole new level of name-calling. For a generation that has been indoctrinated with tolerance messaging, when their toes get stepped on, they are the most intolerant versions of themselves. It's that type of pride that makes us expect the other person to fix things while neglecting any personal responsibility. Of course, that's the message being pushed in this hour, to live for the moment and do what feels good instead of what is right because it's right.

The culture is out of control, and we can't afford to fall into their divisive worldly attitudes, which lead to rebellious ways. "*There is a way that appears to be right, but in the end, it leads to death*" (Proverbs 14:12, NIV). If we follow celebrity culture, we will end up with their results—an over 80 percent divorce rate and the highest incidences of drug/alcohol abuse and early deaths/suicides in the culture. And these are our role models? They're the ones who tell us how to believe and how to vote, what's right and what's wrong? They're supposed to be role models for our lives and children? I don't think so! Yet they are fueling the division they scream against. There are times we disagree with others, but we must disagree with respect.

That's the confusion of the hour. In the last days, people will be lovers of self, lovers of pleasure, lovers of money, abusive, slanderers, disobedient to parents, boastful, and proud. Have you noticed any of this in today's culture? To stay true to God's purpose for our lives, we must divorce celebrity values and realign our beliefs and actions with something higher than paid actors.

I've been married 36 years, have raised a successful family, and experienced solid financial freedom while all along the way struggling to swim upstream—with the culture quick to mow my family down if allowed. Gary and I continue to experience a good life because we didn't take the short route to success through compromise. We were tempted at times, and, yes, there was a price to go against the grain, but I'm grateful we did! Sure, we've made some mistakes along the way, but God has a way of helping us all course correct when we submit our attitudes and humble ourselves before His Word and ways.

Recently, a minister said on social media, "We don't need more truth tellers...." I couldn't disagree more. We do need to tell the truth (with love). It is the truth that sets people free.

Jesus is not *a* way to truth; He is *THE* way.

You and I are called to speak the truth, even when the culture tries to pressure us into silence. *Especially* when the culture tries to pressure us into silence! We must be careful to say the truth with the least offense, but it has to be the truth nonetheless. And expect that it will often be offensive to those who are rebelling against it.

I'm so glad someone told me the truth when I was a mixed-up, young woman headed down a road of destruction. I heard it. I heeded the correction, and today, my life has the fruit of my changed choices.

We must make sure our ways mirror the Word of God if we are going to live free and inherit the blessings of God for our lives. This is not the hour to compromise to keep from getting our feelings hurt. And at the same time, we shouldn't be on a mission to blast people with offensive actions or attitudes.

The enemy is looking for an open door in all of our lives. Getting our feelings hurt and harboring an offense over it is the number one way I know he enters lives—next to blatant disobedience or rebellion.

 Next time you are hurt, don't take to Facebook. Take the following three simple steps:

1. Pray.

2. Forgive.

3. Develop a "plan of communication and restoration."

Our goal should be to represent Jesus in every situation. When I was dealing with sharks, I didn't have the answers, but God did. I would get before the Lord and pray. I would pray, "Father, if there is something that they see that isn't right in me, would you show me so I can change it? I don't want to be blind to any deception. I want to grow and be like you, Jesus. If there's something wrong in the scenario, show me how to handle it. If this is their personal offense, guard my heart from any hurt or offense in this situation."

If you keep your eyes on Jesus and prioritize your walk with Him, you'll build your life on the right foundation. A building that doesn't have a foundation when a storm comes falls, but if you build on Jesus even when things don't look good, even when things aren't right, even when it looks like God's Word has failed you, you're going to see God work in your situation. Don't quit and don't get discouraged. Realize that God is true and His Word is true. He'll never let you down. His hope will not disappoint you.

The decisions you make every day are either building up or tearing down your life. What you meditate on, what you think about, and how you use your time set the course for your future. That's why we have to listen to God! We have to follow His ways because a great building has a deep foundation. God is a good Father. He's not going to let you have a shallow foundation. He's not going to exalt you to do something big if you're going to fall, crumble, and mess up your life under the pressure.

Matthew 7:13-14 (MSG) say, *"Don't look for shortcuts to God. The market is flooded with surefire, easygoing formulas for a successful life that can be practiced in your spare time. Don't fall for that stuff, even though crowds of people do."*

Gary and I lived in an old, beat-up farmhouse for years while God worked with us on our attitudes and how to deal with situations. We had to grow there and learn to trust God, no matter what circumstances came our way. We had to learn to make the *choice* to rejoice.

Success in relationships is a daily process. It's day-to-day encountering sharks, loving people, giving to others, and making the right choices. Pressures come to all of us. My life's not a fairy tale either, but God blesses me, and every day, it becomes more of a fairy tale because I've learned that sharks can't take me if I don't let them. I've learned that God is bigger and better and His blessings are greater than me quitting.

Don't quit! Stay the course, and do what's right!

ACTION ITEMS

Look up Psalm 37:7 in the Bible. What does it say?

_____

_____

_____

Proverbs 37:5 and Proverbs 16:3 tell us to commit our ways to God and He will help us. What are you commiting to God today?

_____

_____

_____

Read Matthew 7:13. What does this verse mean to you?

_____

_____

_____

CHAPTER FOUR:
FOCUS

I used to dread my phone ringing.

Why?

Because I already knew who was calling!

Every day, I had a woman from our church call me to talk about her problems... for *hours.* I was happy to offer my advice and pray with her the first couple of times, but I was starting to notice a pattern... She always called again the next day with the SAME problems. And, to my surprise, she hadn't taken my advice!

I didn't recognize it then, but this woman didn't want help; she wanted an audience. As a leader, one of the most valuable lessons you can learn is the difference between someone who wants help and someone who just wants a handout. I later found out I wasn't the only person getting held up on the phone for hours with this woman. She would talk to me about her problems and then turn around and call somebody else to repeat the same stories!

Being a Christian, I felt like I *had* to talk to her. It would be wrong of me not to, right? My mind-set was so wrong about what being the hands and feet of Jesus really meant. And with that wrong mind-set, I spent every day dreading the sound of my phone ringing.

From the outside looking in, this story may sound unbelievable to you. *How hard is it to just ignore a phone call?* Looking back on it, I totally agree! When you're in the moment, though, things aren't always that clear. The feeling of *obligation* can cause you to make bad decisions for your time, family, and destiny.

Ask yourself: "Are there any unhealthy relationships or situations where I've let *obligation* convince me to jump through hoops or bow down to it?"

There's an unhealthy mind-set in the world that Christians are supposed to be the doormats people walk on, so they never have to step in a puddle. I need you to know this absolutely isn't true. You can't take the place of God in someone's life—nor should you.

In this particular story, being in ministry, I felt it was my moral obligation to take every call I got from this woman and to talk as long as she wanted. In reality, I was *enabling* her to continue down the path she was on! There may have been times in your life, too, that you let sharks gnaw on your hand because you thought it was the "Christian" thing to do. This is a scheme from the enemy to distract you from your destiny!

It's not always DESTRUCTION that keeps us from our destiny; it's DISTRACTION.

Sharks will try to steal your time and intention, but you have to protect your focus. Keep your eyes on Jesus! He will carry you through persecution to victory!

Sharks can try to attack you, but they can't stop you if you refuse to allow your focus to be on them instead of on your mission. You will need to deal with them, but don't let them control the waters! You have a right to swim and get to your promise in God.

Are You Fighting the Right Battle?

Many times, when we do something good or start pursuing God's call on our life, accusations will come against us. Don't be surprised if your success invites criticism from others. When this happens, we have to hold on to God's direction. We can't change course to please people or the naysayers in our life. We have to fight the battle for our destinies, not the battle for *approval*.

Ask yourself: "Which battle have I been fighting?"

We can't sacrifice the will of God for the approval of people. The fact of the matter is there will be times when we have to choose between the two. When Gary and I were trying to get out of debt, we had many friends and family tell us we were taking "this whole get out of debt thing too far." People will criticize the very thing God has called you to do, saying it seems impossible to them, or too hard for them—but that's why God called you to do it, not them.

"Don't expect people to understand your grind when God didn't give them your vision."

—Anonymous

People may not understand what God has called you to do—but down the road, you'll be thankful you stuck with it! And the incredible thing is those same people who discouraged and doubted you will come back and say, "I knew you could do it all along!"

It's tempting when trouble comes to focus on the person who is responsible, to blame, or to become a victim. When criticized, it's a mistake to start doing what someone wants instead of what God said. You can't do it all. You must decide what season you're in and what's important in this season.

This reminds me of a powerful story in Mark 14. In this story, a woman poured expensive perfume over the feet of Jesus and began to wash His feet.

Mark 14:4-9 (NIV) say:

> *Some of those present were saying indignantly to one another, "Why this waste of perfume? It could have been sold for more than a year's wages and the money given to the poor." And they rebuked her harshly. "Leave her alone," said Jesus. "Why are you bothering her? She has done a beautiful thing to me. The poor you will always have with you, and you can help them any time you want. But you will not always have me. She did what she could. She poured perfume on my body beforehand to prepare for my burial. Truly I tell you, wherever the gospel is preached throughout the world, what she has done will also be told, in memory of her."*

Sometimes people will misjudge your heart or what God has called you to do, but it's not between you and them, it's between you and God. When we stay focused on the call of God for our lives, He is able to create a legacy for us beyond anything we could have hoped or imagined!

Refocusing on the Good

When Jesus fed the 5,000, the first question He asked the disciples was, "What do you have?" Right now, you probably have countless opportunities, connections, and potential growth around you waiting for you to seize it. Sometimes we have to get a new perspective and open our minds a little to see it. Someone's going to do it—it might as well be you! The difference between world changers and stagnant drifters comes down to the ability to focus on opportunities, and then seize them.

For years, people enjoyed lunch meat on bread in the comfort of their homes, but two men named Peter Buck and Fred Deluca saw a foot long loaf of bread differently and started a restaurant called Subway. Millions of people saw a sandwich—but Buck and Deluca saw a million dollar corporation. Successful people have the ability to look at ordinary life and see extraordinary potential.

Ask yourself: What areas in my life are working well? What opportunities would I like to focus more on?

_____

_____

_____

POOR THINKING CAN BE SUMMED UP IN FOUR WORDS:

P: PASSING

O: OVER

O: OPPORTUNITIES

R: REGULARLY

Have you ever noticed when children play they don't imagine divorces, or death, or bankruptcy? Children don't make room for failure or low expectations. As adults, it seems *all* many of us do is make room for failure and low expectations... and it costs us our dreams!

I remember asking a little boy at a conference what he wanted to be when he grew up, and I was struck by how quickly he answered the question. He didn't respond with an accountant or a manager at a store. He gave me an extensive LIST of larger-than-life dreams—a firefighter, an astronaut, a policeman, and a monster truck driver. There was nothing "practical" about his career goals. There wasn't a glimpse of fear or discouragement when he said them either.

When Jesus said we should have faith like a child, I believe this is what He meant. Children don't make room for failure. They're "possibility-thinkers." They see a world full of doors opening up before them, overflowing with opportunities.

Ask yourself: "Have I diligently been searching for opportunities? Am I thinking big enough?"

_____

_____

_____

You have what you need right now to build a beautiful life; you just have to open your eyes and see the possibilities in front of you. Life asks multiple choice questions. If you can't see all of your options, you're not thinking big enough!

ACTION ITEMS

I want you to grab a piece of paper and a pen, set a timer for five minutes, and write down every opportunity that you can think of. Possible connections, projects, business start-ups, books you could write, blogs you could start, time you could use better, properties you could own, activities you and your children could do. Nothing is too big or too small for your list. If it's something you want to focus on over the next year, write it down!

Here are some examples:

"Call Susan and see if she will sell my product in her store."

"Hire a virtual assistant."

"Drive by investment properties in my area."

"Grab coffee with someone who is doing what I aspire to do."

"Take a class on time management."

"Outline the book I want to write"

"Start a weekly blog."

"Compile my recipes into a cookbook."

"Ask to speak at my daughter's class."

The *opportunities* are endless!

To make this process easier for you, I've compiled a short list of "mental triggers" to help you brainstorm outside of the box. Read each word on this list, and write down any ideas that come to mind. If you can't think of anything, move to the next item on the list. This is an optional tool to help you focus, be more thorough, and possibly come up with concepts you never would have considered.

Remember, the key is that we're changing our mind-sets! We're becoming possibility-thinkers. And when we look at our world through a lens of opportunity, we see things that the rest of the world misses. Big things. Important things.

BUSINESS OPPORTUNITIES:

Books to read

Marketing strategies

Advertising campaigns

Items to discuss with a coach

Successful people to reach out to

Mentors

Networking

Coffee dates

Self-improvement

Referrals

Retail opportunities

Real estate

Connections

Budgets

Investments

TIME OPPORTUNITIES:

Activities to quit

Activities to join

Organizational changes

Delegation

Email

Social media

Phones

Priorities

SKILL OPPORTUNITIES:

Hobbies	Blogs
Creative projects	Health
Passions	Fitness
Classes to take	Stress management
Areas to become an expert in	
Books	

Have your list? Great! Take a second and look over it. You probably have a few items where you thought, "I could be onto something here!" You may also have some that struck the thought, "This one isn't worth much…." Don't worry about it. You never know when you'll find a gold coin in a fish's mouth.

You'll want to revisit the rest of your list later, but to start, pick the three ideas that make your heart skip a beat. These ideas need to be something you can act on right away and that show signs of potential.

Now, you have a two-week deadline to act on these opportunities. Practice applying the discipline of *focus*.

Pull out your calendar and schedule a time to follow up on each idea. If you have the time now, go ahead and start. If it's an idea that's going to take time to implement, schedule it out. Put an hour aside on your calendar every day to make progress—write, exercise, read, or make calls. The important thing is that you act *URGENTLY*. I believe many people will find themselves in heaven one day amazed to discover how many million-dollar ideas God gave them that they didn't value, cultivate, or focus on. God can show you where to capture the fish, but you have to cast the net.

CHAPTER FIVE:
FEAR NOT

The invitation was unexpected.

I had been asked to attend a Joyce Meyer Women's Conference, with a "greenroom" invite. The opportunity was both delightful and terrifying. Of course, being familiar with the ministry of Joyce, the notion of meeting her face-to-face was a genuine thrill. But, being a newcomer to the world of TV, I was clueless about "Greenrooms." I had no idea that it was merely a backstage area where those "on the stage" gathered with friends and invited guests. It was simply a convenient place to meet, greet, and snack on potato chips.

When I eventually arrived and crossed the threshold into the room, I was immediately met by Joyce. As she shook my hand warmly, a sudden wave of intimidation overtook me, and I realized that the only thing actually "green" in that room was—ME. In that unfamiliar setting, I was the novice, the rookie, petrified by my surroundings. Never had I felt so totally out of place!

Nervously glancing around the room, recognizing faces from television and talk shows, my mind swirled, "What am I doing here? I'm nobody. Why would anyone talk to me? ...I have to sit down."

Spotting an empty chair, I slumped next to another pastor's wife who looked just as frightened as I did. As the room filled, we two sat alone, silent and intimidated. People eventually borrowed chairs from our otherwise empty table. Then Joyce walked past us into an adjacent room. My eyes followed.

I didn't realize it till it was too late, but in my daze, I found myself staring, fixating on Joyce. Unconsciously, I tracked her through the room as if glued to one of her on-screen programs. No doubt feeling my unintentional intrusion, our eyes met. And with a subtle wave of her hand, she directed the private conversation she was having away from my gawking gaze.

"Oh, great!" I whispered to myself. "She saw me!" Embarrassment flushed my cheeks, and I wanted to melt into the shiny polished floors. I prayed she would forget my face.

Intimidation isn't pretty. It compels you to compare yourself to everything and everyone else. That harsh eye-opening evaluation can be overwhelming and debilitating. It can stop you in your tracks and chain you to that one moment you'd just rather forget. Intimidation is you convincing yourself that you don't measure up. And *"as he thinks in his heart, so is he"* (Proverbs 23:7, NKJV).

That sense of inferiority is just another word for fear. And fear is simply the self-deception that you are about to be separated from the thing you *most* value. And in that greenroom moment, what I valued most was my self-esteem. Having been thrust into a new world of opportunity and ministry, I felt like a Hawaiian-shirted, camera-toting tourist, gawking at the scenery, taking wide-eyed mental snapshots of every famous face that walked by.

We've all been there. We have all felt that awkward, out of place, don't-know-what-to-do-or-say feeling. And though everything that happens to us can be a moment of instruction, we are often too overwhelmed or self-absorbed to take the lesson to heart.

So the lesson comes around again.

About a year after that greenroom adventure, my husband and I received another invitation, this time to join Joyce Meyer as guests on her program. Again, it was a thrill. But before I could get too excited about the possibilities, my mind flashed back to the embarrassment of that crowded, not so green room.

Yes, I was stuck *there,* at that enormous, chair-less table for two, hoping that my rude, rookie stares had been cast into the Sea of Joyce's Forgetfulness. Thinking otherwise made me a little nauseous, and I contemplated "getting sick" or disappearing quietly before the program. Yes, the human part of me was being itself, in other words—SELFish.

Intimidation keeps your mind on you and conveys that image to others.

When I realized that, I flashed on the image of the thousands who watch Joyce's program daily—women, *like me,* looking for an escape from their own self-images, looking for their purposes, their places in the world. In that moment, realizing that I had BEEN THERE, DONE THAT, the repetitive lessons of my experience finally came into sharp focus.

Like every woman, I have a voice. Combined with my acquired biblical knowledge and life experience, I have accumulated the influence and persuasion necessary to connect with women out there who are just like me.

After the greenroom, the last thing I wanted to do was face Joyce and her vast TV audience, but when I realized that my experience and my voice were perfectly tuned to that very audience, I decided to be brave—to step onto that TV set, next to Joyce, deliberately stare into the eye of the camera, and share my passion for others' success.

That act of getting my SELF out of the way and focusing on the needs of others became the catalyst for everything thereafter.

Eventually, I was offered a program of my own. After sharing my heart and my rags to riches, hurting feminist to mother of five story, the ABC Network offered me a position on their network. And ironically, the time slot they offered was just "next door" to Joyce Meyer's program!

When intimidation closes in on you like the four walls of a greenroom, remember: You were invited there by God. You may not think you're worthy to rub shoulders with "the next level," but God has a program for you. And when you put fear aside, become brave enough to see past your own SELF evaluation and put the needs of others first, God will give you a time slot, and... an experienced mentor who's just "next door"!

ACTION ITEMS

Have you ever let intimidation hold you back from your dreams?

_____

_____

_____

_____

Read 2 Timothy 1:7. What does this verse mean to you?

_____

_____

_____

_____

What is one area where you would like to be more brave?

_____

_____

_____

_____

Look up Deuteronomy 31:6. What does it say?

_____

_____

_____

_____

CHAPTER SIX:
SIX SIGNS YOU'RE SHARK BAIT

Have *you* ever been shark bait?

We all like to think we're the masters of our lives and that we don't allow ourselves to be manipulated or controlled by anyone. However, that's rarely the case. If we could recognize when we're becoming shark bait, maybe we wouldn't find ourselves there as often as we do! That's the issue. In most cases, we become shark bait by taking false responsibility. We think there is something *we're* doing wrong, so we try to perform and jump through hoops for people.

Here are some telltale symptoms we experience when we're being manipulated by sharks:

1. We don't get out of the boat.

Dread is often a symptom of being shark bait. I remember a time when I experienced *dread* every time I had to speak or step out in my calling. I felt like I couldn't do anything right! And the reason why? I dreaded hearing the opinion of a specific woman who always gave me her two cents worth on how I did. We were "friends," so I thought she had my best interests at heart. Thinking she was a friend, I didn't recognize the sharklike relationship I was feeding. That is, until it got to the point where I felt like quitting!

I remember talking to Gary one day and saying, "*They're* going to think..."

My husband interrupted kindly. "Honey, who's *they?*"

I finally took a step back and realized this friend's criticism was a huge source of anxiety in my life. Did that sound like a healthy friendship? Of course not!

You see, when a shark has influence in your life, it makes you want to stay in the boat. They make you feel intimidated, trapped, can take the fun out of your calling, and, ultimately, make you want to quit or give up. If you feel dread doing the things you used to love, or harbor anxiety toward a specific friend's reaction every time you do something, you may want to reconsider that friendship. They either don't have your best interests at heart, or they are simply unaware of the negative patterns they have fallen into.

When you step out of the boat, there will be people who tell you it's impossible. You will sink if you try that! There are dangers if you dare to venture outside the norm. Stay in the boat if you want to be secure. If you choose to be controlled by these voices instead of by the Holy Spirit, fear will dominate your life, and so will the people who exercise this power over your thoughts, actions, and destiny. The greatest loss is the loss of one's calling because we were listening to the wrong voices. Conquering can give you courage. Courage is a heart matter. The actual word comes from the word "Coeur" meaning heart. We must have heart and overcome if we are to thrive in life and not merely survive!

2. We don't try anymore.

The second symptom we experience is self-doubt. Sharks make us feel like we aren't capable, so we should just give up before we even try. When a shark has influence in your life, you may find yourself quick to turn down opportunities, and afraid you'll invite their criticism and upset the waters. Self-doubt is like poison—if we tolerate it, even just a little, it will kill our confidence and can even make us feel paralyzed.

3. We give up on our dreams and callings.

"The only thing wrong with trying to please everyone is that there's always at least one person who will remain unhappy— You."

—Elizabeth Parker

After dread and self-doubt consume us, we often surrender our dreams at the altar of fear. We don't think we'll ever make it. We can't deal with the people, we wish we could change something about ourselves, or it just seems downright impossible. We start to settle for what sharks tell us we can do and have. My friend, only God can tell you what you can do, who you are, and what you have through Him!

How do we fall into unhealthy patterns and take false responsibility for people or the shark who abuses others? In Dr. C. Thomas and Maureen Anderson's book, *Name of the Game of Life*, Maureen Anderson discusses three different roles of dysfunctional patterns originating from parental examples and life experiences. These three roles are the victim, the enabler, and the persecutor. The traits of these roles help us to see how we can assume unhealthy attitudes and fall into the sin of idolatry, greed, or legalism in relationships. These are unhealthy ways in which people relate to and use one another to meet needs that only God can fill. Here are a few traits of these three roles:

VICTIM – demanding, immature emotionally, difficulty in dealing with responsibility, seldom holds job long, feels insecure, needs taken care of, you can never do enough for them, turns on those who help and blames them if they stop helping; competes with leaders to build their own kingdom; often suicidal and/or sick when in trouble.

ENABLER – feels overly responsible for others and attempts to save them; guilt, anxiety, lives for others, and overloaded with problem people; people pleaser, identity comes from fixing people, feels guilt about self-care, self-imposed pressure, martyr, and feels unappreciated.

PERSECUTOR – no compassion for weakness, critical, controlling, combative, creates crisis, all-knowing authority, worrier, perfectionist.

I have a good friend that spent her life trying to get approval by allowing herself to be used and often abused by people. She became a people pleaser because she so badly wanted the attention and affirmation she didn't receive from a father while growing up. As a small child, his absence created feelings of rejection, abandonment, and false responsibility that she was the reason. Her mother, on the other hand, handled her own rejection and low self-worth by criticizing her; she thought it would help her daughter try hard to be worthy of the love she didn't experience. This made the daughter try harder and harder to be perfect. Her mother became the persecutor.

As the young woman grew, she went through cycle after cycle of performing for love for both her parents. The father (victim) expected they both would give in to his demands because he felt life had been unfair to him and everyone owed him. She eventually grew into a very insecure woman who feared living without love. She worked without stopping to please everyone, enabling others. When this didn't work, she started criticizing the ungrateful people she performed for and assisted. Eventually, she chose to be a victim herself, wounded and bitter, feeling that because of her emptiness someone owed her. One day, she came to the end of this impossible mixed-up pursuit. Jesus was there and offered to help her. She decided to spend her life receiving His love, allowing Him to free her from fear and heal her wounds. Today she has become a helper to others and is no longer an enabler, persecutor, or victim. She loves and shares truth with those that will listen and then lets others decide what they want for themselves. She is free!

Jesus was none of the negative roles listed above; He was the helper.

HELPER – never enables others to sin; helps those who truly want help; makes people accountable for their own actions; calls people to have faith for themselves; never controls or manipulates; never forces people to change; doesn't take false responsibility; encourages; loves; pleases God and calls people to maturity.

Jesus helped meet people's needs while holding them accountable for their own decisions. He did not assume false responsibility for people's sin or choices. "Go and sin no more lest a worse thing happen," "Sell your possessions, give to the poor and come follow me," were decisions He placed squarely on the shoulders of the person responsible. When they chose to do something different, He didn't chase them down and try to force them to comply. Our goal should be to live and relate to others as Jesus did, to be willing and open to serve someone in need but not to enable them to depend on us but, rather, to build their lives on Him.

Do you see any unhealthy patterns in your life?

4. We live for the approval of others.

"We must not confuse the command to love with the disease to please."

—Lysa TerKeurst

In Melissa Dahl's article *The People Who See Monsters in the Mirror*, she interviewed several girls about what they saw in the mirror.

"Everyone else, everyone, is beautiful," Lucy said. "I just feel that I am that one ugly person ... I see myself as lower than everyone else."

Louise felt so uncomfortable with the way she looks, she said, "I just can't get to the point where I feel good enough to be able to go out and let anyone see me."

Many people have similar feelings of unworthiness that affect their days, even if they aren't quite as extreme. I've been there, done that, got the T-shirt—and I know it's not God's best for you!

I spent most of my younger years in search of acceptance—from people, from my family, and from myself. I wasn't really sure what I was looking for. What made a woman worth loving? Was it how a woman walked, or how she dressed, or some secret knowledge she possessed that gave her an edge over other women? Whatever it was, I couldn't seem to obtain it. I was constantly changing myself and buying into the new image the culture sold me, but in the end ... I was still just "me." My quest to find an answer for the question, "*Who am I?*" kept me chasing after the culture's elusive remedies.

I remember looking at myself in the mirror as a young girl with tears swelling in my eyes. I pointed a finger at my reflection and started to shout, "*I hate you! I hate you! I hate you!*" I couldn't calm myself down.

Every time I looked at my reflection, I saw imperfections too horrible for anyone to love.

I decided that since I wasn't pretty, I would make up for it by being smart. I would work harder and perform more to be worth something. That insecurity drove me to radical feminism and people pleasing to the point that I couldn't enjoy being around my family or friends anymore.

Trying to find myself in the culture was like trying to find the gold at the end of the rainbow. No matter how hard I looked, I could never find what I was looking for. I crashed through relationships like a tornado. I had a lot of dreams for my life, but I was constantly searching for my value, and I was always frustrated with where I was going.

I was miserable.

Not only was I miserable, but also I was bitter and hard to be around. I thought that I hated the people who hurt me, but I really hated myself. I hated my flaws. I hated anything that might remind me that I was unlovable. Desperate, I cried out to God for His help.

A friend invited me to a church service, and by that point, I was searching to find the missing piece in my life. I agreed to go, and at the end of the service, *I rededicated my heart to God.*

Acts 5:29 (ESV) says, "*But Peter and the apostles answered, 'We must obey God rather than men.'*"

If we are living for the approval of others, we aren't living for the approval of God. Period! Matthew 6:24 (NIV) says, "*No one can serve two masters. Either you will hate the one and love the other, or you will be devoted to the one and despise the other.*"

You only need one approval, and that's God's!

"If you live for people's acceptance, you will die from their rejection."

—**Lecrae Moore**

If you have to perform for people's approval, trust me, it's not worth having. They may love you today, but the moment you let them down, they'll turn against you. Trust God and follow His will for your life! His love is *unconditional*.

5. We don't take risks. Instead, we live safe lives not doing what we really want.

I know people that won't go into the ocean because they're afraid of sharks. I also know people who won't go for their destinies, that won't step out and be the best they can be, because they're afraid of the criticism of other people. They're afraid of getting hurt, or that someone's not going to understand them or like them. Maybe they've stepped out before, and someone lashed out at them, so they're not going to try anymore. They're afraid to be themselves, so they spend their lives being somebody they're not!

Do you know anybody like that? Have you ever been guilty of that? I know I have!

I started as that woman. I was very insecure and very fearful of what people thought of me. The fear of man was paralyzing to me because I wanted to be accepted so badly. I tied all of my worth and value to what someone else said about me. I have had to face me and deal with the root of these challenges before I could face my future with certainty that I could win, and that it's God's plan I do.

6. We retreat. Feel defeat. Repeat (every time we take a step and get bit, we retreat).

Have you ever heard the expression, *"One step forward, two steps back"*?

Sharks can make us feel that way!

We get excited about the territory we're taking for the Kingdom, but after talking to somebody about it and hearing their doubt, we start to feel discouraged. We allow the opinions of *people* to change our opinion of our victories!

Have you experienced any of these symptoms in your life? Have you ever felt dread, fear, or self-doubt because of a person's influence over you?

We all have, but don't worry... Through Christ, you can become *shark proof!*

ACTION ITEMS

Has there ever been a time where you experienced these symptoms in your life? What happened?

_____

_____

_____

_____

Can you identify any toxic relationships in your life right now? How can you deal with these situations moving forward?

_____

_____

_____

_____

Read Acts 5:29. What does this verse mean to you?

_____

_____

_____

_____

PART TWO:
HOW TO RECOGNIZE
A SHARK

CHAPTER SEVEN:
THE FIVE SHARK MANEUVERS

Through years of dealing with people in business and ministry, I have discovered five tactics we face when dealing with people en route to our dreams. As we go through these common maneuvers, don't forget: good people can do bad things when they are hurting. I'm not sharing this list to make you think everyone is conspiring against you, secretly plotting your demise with five-step plans. Any one of us can be a perpetrator or a recipient of these maneuvers if we aren't wise. Often, people do these things unknowingly, simply responding with habits and reactions they've learned. Negative emotions like fear, anger, jealousy, insecurity, and bitterness are frequently the root problem that inspires them.

Matthew 10:16 (NIV) says, "I am sending you out like sheep among wolves. **Therefore be as shrewd as snakes and as innocent as doves**." We must be wise to the schemes of the enemy—meanwhile, still loving people and recognizing it's not flesh and blood we're dealing with. The good news is you don't have to spend your life bowing down to these tactics, constantly stitching yourself up from shark attack after shark attack. You can learn to safely swim with the sharks!

SHARK MANEUVER #1:
Fear and Intimidation

TACTIC: Scare tactics and power plays

GOAL: To gain control over you and intimidate you from being more successful than them

COMMON ROOT ISSUE: Inferiority

Fear and intimidation is the most common and easy shark attack to fall prey to. In the water, this kind of shark attack is called the "bump-and-bite." This is when the shark swims around its prey, hitting it with its body or head before attacking. It aims to strike fear, intimidation, and confusion in you before it attacks, and it allows the animal to discover if you'll fight back.

My husband and I went to Oral Roberts University before we got married. We applied ourselves in school and believed God that we would have a business one day. We wanted to have a hand in business so we could preach the Gospel and share the truth of the Word of God without judgment—without fear of somebody saying, "If you don't share this, we're going to cut your paycheck." We didn't want to be controlled by people; we wanted God to be able to lead us. So we started a business. After 10 years of overseeing employees and sales teams, we had some experience working with people under our belt. Then God called us to start a church. In the early days of our ministry, Gary and I expected everything to be a breeze. After all, we had been in the cutthroat business world for years now. *Christians are supposed to love everyone, right? How hard could working with them be?*

I thought when we stepped out to pastor a church it was going to be so much easier than running a business... You know what I discovered? There are sharks everywhere. Anywhere there are people, there are going to be sharks.

A few years after the church started, I encountered one of my first sharks in ministry. A woman—let's call her Rubie—came to church and made it her personal mission to take over our women's ministry. I had been running it at the time, but I was timid and insecure in my ability. I was new to preaching, and my fear of public speaking made me dread speaking to the large group of women every time our events came around. It didn't help that Rubie began to consistently tell me the ways I was failing. She always had pointers for me when I was done preaching. Not only that, but she was constantly criticizing my husband and me and the things we were doing in the ministry. Instead of *supporting* the church, she was trying to *compete* with the church.

Unfortunately, I didn't understand the authority God had trusted me with. If you don't protect and respect the authority God has given you and you allow people to intimidate you, whether it's in your job, in your relationships, or in your family, those same people will take your position from you and use it against you.

Sharks aim to intimidate you and make you feel like you can't do what God has called you to do. Just because they're intimidating, don't be afraid! When it comes down to it, most of the time they're jealous and want what you have. Some of them are malicious; some of them just haven't discovered their identities.

I'm sorry to say I jumped through hoops to make Rubie happy for *far* too long. At one point, I got invited to speak at a women's conference, and I excitedly agreed. I invited all of the women who attended our church to attend as well... and that's when I did something really stupid.

Have you ever found yourself doing something that was not in your best interest, or your family's best interest, because you were intimidated by someone?

Well, that's exactly what I did!

The night of the women's conference, Rubie called me. "My babysitter cancelled tonight," she said without a hint of disappointment slipping through her voice. "So, Gary can babysit my kids tonight while I'm at the conference."

It wasn't a question; it was a fact. I was so intimidated to stand up to her, I stupidly said, "Of course he will! No problem!" I called my husband and told him the exciting news... I had booked him to babysit all evening.

Oh boy, I had so much to learn as a leader. But wait, it gets worse... Guess what Gary and I did *next?*

We gave Rubie a position in the church because we thought *that* would make her happy!

Of course, that only made things a million times worse because now she had authority to throw around. I'm sad to admit that we put up with this for years, until something happened that forced us to confront her. When we finally had to confront her, we did it nicely; we told her how much we loved her, all we felt God wanted for her, and then we shared the things that needed to change. I never expected what happened next...

She left the church!

I thought to myself, "*What was I protecting all of those years? Obviously her heart wasn't for us; she left after one small correction!*"

I had to learn to make the decision as a leader to be strong in the Lord and the power of His might. Unless you break away from the intimidation and control of sharks, you will never rise above them!

God didn't want that woman to be a shark. He placed me as a leader in her life to help her by telling her the truth and confronting what was in her. Instead, I was too cowardly to do it. I don't want you to be cowardly! I want you to deal with what you need to deal with so that you can grow, so that others can grow, and so that we can all walk in unity.

I love the latest movie interpretation of Cinderella. Cinderella's mother gives her some powerful advice: "Have courage, and be kind." Courage and kindness—those are two dynamic ingredients for a great life! You're going to have to be courageous if you're going to swim with sharks. You're going to have to be courageous if you're going to be the person that God's called you to be. When a shark begins circling you and "bumping" you to see if you'll fall prey to fear and intimidation, it's critical that you maintain your authority. Second Timothy 1:7 (NIV) encourages us, *"For the Spirit God gave us does not make us timid, but gives us power, love and self-discipline."* Be bold! Be courageous! God's grace is backing you!

SHARK MANEUVER #2:
Exploiting Weaknesses

TACTIC: Identify weaknesses in leaders and capitalize on them

GOAL: To find reluctant, timid, or insecure leaders and manipulate them for personal gain

COMMON ROOT ISSUE: Pride

Similar to the fear and intimidation line of attack, this maneuver looks for weakness to strike. This kind of shark will take as much ground as you give him, and the more you cower down to please it, the more it demands. These sharks can smell a drop of blood a mile away. They love to find reluctant, timid, or insecure leaders and gain control over them.

My family has always been a big fan of the *Lord of the Rings* movie trilogy. When I look at this shark attack, I'm reminded of a scene from the second movie, *The Two Towers*. It's a scene between King Theoden, the king of Rohan, and Wormtongue, his royal adviser. King Theoden is a good king, but he is a reluctant leader. Wormtongue has spotted this weakness and begun to manipulate, control, and force his will onto King Theoden. In the movies, the control Wormtongue has gained over King Theoden shows in his appearance—Theoden has white, glazed-over eyes, long, straggly white hair, and he can barely grunt a word. He still sits on the throne, but he doesn't run his kingdom anymore. Wormtongue does.

How many leaders allow somebody to usurp their authority and control them the same way King Theoden did?

This story has a happy ending though! Gandalf arrives at Rohan and liberates King Theoden from Wormtongue's evil control, and Theoden is able to take back his authority over the kingdom. At this point, we see an incredible transformation in King Theoden—his hair turns brown, his eyes regain their color, wrinkles disappear, and he looks 30 years younger. This scene shows a powerful visual picture of what happens when we allow somebody to gain control over our lives!

In the early days of the church, I wanted everybody to love me. I thought if somebody didn't love me, it was absolutely my fault. I thought it must have been an indication of something I needed to change, or something I needed to adapt to. So every time something went wrong, I changed. I started letting myself get boxed in! Before long, I was so wrapped up in the opinions of others, I wasn't free to live. I felt like I was walking on eggshells in a lot of the relationships in my life. Gary would see it and encourage me to let go of those relationships, but I would defend them. The crazy part was, instead of pulling away from those toxic relationships, I leaned into them even more! I tried to jump through hoops to make them like me more. I spent more time trying to make the people who *didn't* like me love me than I did with the people who were on my team from day one.

Why do we try to look for sharks? Why do we try to please the sharks that hurt us, hold us back, and keep us from our destinies?

Did you know that sharks have suckerfish that follow them around and suck the dead skin cells off of them and eat their feces?

Gross? I know!

Listen. You don't want to be the suckerfish that sucks all of the dead skin off of the sharks. For too many years, I was that suckerfish—following the sharks around, trying to get them to like me, and trying to do what they wanted me to do instead of what God *told* me to do. I was being who they wanted me to be instead of who God created me to be. The only thing those suckerfish do is eat… well, feces. And guess what the shark does in the long run? Eventually, he turns and eats the suckerfish!

In the early years of my life, I never confronted or dealt with the sharks in my life. I surrendered to them and let them bleed me dry. One thing I've learned about sharks is that if you see a shark coming for you, you can't get scared. You can't back down. You can't *please* a shark. You have to stand your ground!

Don't be a sucker!

Sharks look for weakness. They want you to bow down to them. Or like the sharks and those suckerfish, they want you to serve their purpose until they don't need you anymore. If you allow sharks to dictate your decisions, they will try to exert their will on you more and more. Like a drop of blood in the ocean, sharks from all over the place will come swarming.

God has called us to love people, to be an example, and to be kind, but we have to take courage and be wise because there are sharks out there. We don't need to be fearful of sharks, but we *do* need to have an awareness of them.

Satan wants to use sharks to move you from your purpose. Don't let him!

We don't need to look at our mistakes and become self-focused. We need to be focused on Jesus and what He's done, what He's already finished. We all have a Savior who died for us and says we're worthy, we're valuable, we're acceptable, we're unique, and we're created for something special. You can look at Jesus and say, "I'm righteous because of what He did, and because of that, I can hold my head up high. My identity is in Christ, and I don't have to be moved by any sharks. I don't have to become a sucker... I can be who God created me to be!"

SHARK MANEUVER #3:
Hidden Motives

TACTIC: Betrayal

GOAL: To get what they want at the cost of others

COMMON ROOT ISSUE: Jealousy

This is the most deadly shark attack that exists—it's rooted deep in the kind of betrayal that cuts a leader to their very core. Like a great white does, this shark attack comes by surprise and aims to draw blood.

Sharks often have ulterior motives and selfish intentions behind their actions. We had a sweet family in our church—let's call them the "Smiths"—who were approached by a couple in a financial bind. This couple befriended them and confided in them about how deeply in debt they were, and how they were about to lose their house. The Smiths felt bad and wished there was something they could do to help their new friends. When the Smiths inherited a large sum of money from a relative's passing, they generously gave thousands of dollars to the couple in financial trouble to get right on their house… A few months later, to their surprise, the couple lost their house despite the money they had given to them! The fallout between the two families was catastrophic. And just like that, the Smiths and this couple's friendship was over.

This story is a great example of a common tactic sharks use. A shark's friendship, loyalty, or love is often two-faced. They befriend people and do nice things, but they do it with ulterior motives. They may

SHARK PROOF How to Deal with Difficult People

flatter you because you have a nice title at work, hoping you'll put in a good word for them. Or perhaps they befriend you for your connections or name. However, when it comes down to it, a shark has zero loyalty. Once they have what they want or a better offer comes along, they're gone as quickly as they appeared.

Judas demonstrated this sharklike quality when he betrayed Jesus. He was one of Jesus's disciples, mentoring under Him and ministering with Him. Unfortunately, Judas had selfish ulterior motives. He was self-seeking; he didn't have any loyalty to Jesus. When a price was put on Jesus's head, Judas betrayed Him for the money. To make more of a mockery of their friendship, Judas even betrayed Him with a kiss! Matthew 26:48-50 (NIV) say, *"Now the betrayer had arranged a signal with them: 'The one I kiss is the man; arrest him.' Going at once to Jesus, Judas said, 'Greetings, Rabbi!' and kissed him. Jesus replied, 'Do what you came for, friend.' Then the men stepped forward, seized Jesus and arrested him."*

Have you ever experienced this kind of betrayal in leadership?

As a leader in today's culture, it's unlikely you'll encounter a friend who will sell you to the authorities to be killed, but that doesn't mean you can't relate. I have heard story after story of this kind of stinging betrayal from a shark. In fact, Gary and I have experienced it firsthand on several occasions! This is the deepest kind of betrayal. There is nothing as painful or devastating as this tactic from the enemy. I can trace any time Gary and I have been tempted to quit to this type of attack! These attacks can be especially hurtful when they come from someone you love and trust—someone in your inner circle, like Judas was to Jesus. It may come from a staff member, a close friend, or even a family member.

The worst part is you can't always avoid this kind of shark attack.

Even Jesus, who was a perfect leader, experienced betrayal in His team. That's actually good news! People may betray you, but you don't need to take it personally. Jesus was a *perfect* leader, remember? A person's betrayal is not a reflection on you as a leader, it's a reflection of what's going on in them. You can pray for them, but stay the course! It's not flesh and blood we're dealing with. Don't turn from your assignment. Don't jump through hoops and sacrifice your calling in life to please people.

I think too many leaders spend half of their lives trying to keep their Judas from hanging himself instead of hanging out with the eleven who could help further their mission!

According to Dag Heward-Mills's book *Loyalty and Disloyalty*, these are the eight stages of disloyalty:

1. Independent Spirit

Heward-Mills says, "When a person belonging to a group, ministry or company develops an independent attitude, he sort of becomes autonomous within the set-up. The rules of the organization no longer control him."

2. Offense

A person who is in the offended stage begins to meditate on their hurt, nurturing bitterness, suspicion, and even hatred.

3. Passivity

Heward-Mills says, "When a person is in the passive stage of the disloyalty process he does not involve himself in much. He sits and watches unconcerned and uninvolved."

4. The Critical Stage

"A disloyal person is not passive forever; he progresses into the next step of being critical. This is the stage of noticing and magnifying faults."

5. Political Stage

Then comes the political stage. According to Heward-Mills, "When a person becomes political, he tries to involve others in his ideas and philosophies." He is gathering a following that verify his offenses and misperceptions. The person finds great delight in being the "enlightened one" and enjoys the attention of the followers.

6. Deception

At this point, the person is totally deceived and convinced they are right and the leader is wrong. This total deception now leads the person to the final stages.

7. Open Rebellion

The rebellion that once was hidden is now open rebellion. The deceived person makes their play for authority, usually with many casualties.

8. Mutiny

All rebels fall in the end. The foundation of their power was built on rebellion, and they will all fall from rebellion. Very quickly, those that have followed find fault in their new leader and follow the same path of destruction that they were trained in, and the cycle repeats itself.

SHARK MANEUVER #4:
Control and Authority Issues

TACTIC: Attack the reputation and credibility of authorities

GOAL: To elevate themselves as an authority in the eyes of others

COMMON ROOT ISSUE: Rebellion

In the early days of our church, we had a couple loudly interrupt service to give a prophetic word. We had never seen them before. Nobody knew who they were. Gary and I introduced ourselves to the couple after service and nicely encouraged them to plug in for a while before giving words during service, or to go to the elders first. They agreed. A few weeks later, the wife asked me out to dinner because she had something she needed to talk to me about. Of course, I happily accepted her invitation. Little did I know I was in for one of the most interesting lunches of my life.

I arrived at lunch hungry and unaware of what I was walking into. I thought we'd exchange some friendly chat, I'd be a listening ear for some problem she was facing, and we'd go our merry ways an hour and a half later. To my surprise, we weren't there to discuss any problems she was facing... we were there to discuss my problems!

"I have a word for you," she started, her expression somber. "Your husband is controlling you. He's stifling your gifts."

"Wait, what now?" I blurted, trying to keep an edge from creeping into my tone.

"It's clear you don't even have your own email."

I was stunned into silence. After I picked my jaw up off of the table, I forced a response. "I'm sorry; I think you misunderstood him. My husband isn't controlling at *all*. I don't have my own email because I don't want one! I'm home with my kids most of the week. I don't want to have to worry about keeping up with an email right now."

Her face scrunched up in shock. "You're in *denial*," she said. "Your husband is misusing your gifts!"

The lunch only went downhill from there. Despite my continuous defense of Gary, she continued to build me up and tear Gary down. We ended the lunch with me chuckling and saying, "I don't know what else to tell you," and her making one last insistence that I was in denial. To top the already terrible dinner, she stuck me with the bill.

After that lunch, the couple stopped attending our church, offended. A few months later, Gary and I went out to dinner, and to our surprise, we found ourselves seated by none other than this couple. They were eating with a young man. We were close enough that I could overhear some of their conversation, and I couldn't believe my ears! It sounded so similar to the speech the wife had given me when *we* went out to lunch! After they were done eating, they stuck the young man with the bill.

A year later, Gary and I got a call from this couple. They explained they had moved to Alabama to start a church, and it was going terrible. They were behind on their rent and in desperate need of money. They didn't understand why God had failed them.

Sharks often go after authorities and their reputations because they are jealous of the respect, power, position, prosperity, and promotion of those who have paid a price to succeed. Their accusations may make them look like the innocent victim, but, in reality, they are out for blood.

When sharks go after an authority, they often slather it in shameless flattery, just like that woman did with me at lunch. They can execute this combination so well that you may not even notice the rebellion under the surface. You'll hear them say cunning things like:

"I would never do that."

"I wish *you* were leading this project. You would be a much better boss."

"You're way more talented than they are."

Satan *hates* authority, so it's no wonder he loves to wage war against it! Romans 13:1 (NIV) says, "*Let everyone be subject to the governing authorities, for there is no authority except that which God has established. The authorities that exist have been established by God.*"

Sharks are clever—when you agree with their flattery, you become a signature on their petition. If they come to you and talk bad about your boss and you agree, they'll go to the next person and tell them that *you* have issues with your boss, and use your name to stir up more people toward their cause. You never win when you put your hand in a shark's mouth.

Many years ago, a woman who attended our church rented a meeting room in an inn to throw a birthday party for her husband. Gary and I happily attended, and we had a great evening spending time with friends over dinner. At the end of the evening, the wife hosting the party called Gary over to a private conversation. "I threw this party by faith... I don't have the money to pay for it," she told him. "Can you pay for it?"

We ended up paying for the room rental and all of the guests' dinners. It wasn't cheap! If you don't know how to say no and set boundaries, sharks will learn how to control and manipulate you to get their desired outcome.

I remember one Sunday morning back in the very beginning of our church, a lady approached my husband and me to discuss all of my problems and the things I was doing wrong.

"I quit!" I blurted. "I quit! I can't do this anymore. I can't put up with this anymore. I'm not the right person for this job."

My husband looked shocked. "You can't quit, Drenda; you're my wife. I need you by my side."

He eventually talked me back to my right senses. Thinking back now, I can't imagine what would have happened if I had actually quit that day—if I had allowed a shark to convince me to give up on what God had called me to do!

Yikes.

If you let sharks call the shots, control, and manipulate you, it will lead you down a road of burnout, hopelessness, and even depression. You know why? Because you were never created to please *people*; you were created to please God. You have to protect your authority and boundaries from sharks!

SHARK MANEUVER #5:
Sharks Find Sharks

TACTIC: Gossip and stir up offense

GOAL: To justify their offenses by passing them on to others

COMMON ROOT ISSUE: Bitterness

Sharks find strength in numbers. They have an "angry mob" mentality and love the justification they feel to have a group of people backing them. They never take a problem lying down. When a shark feels they have been wronged or didn't get their way, they quickly begin passing out the torches and pitchforks to anyone standing by. They start spreading blood in the water, trying to draw a crowd. I like to call it going into "campaign mode." These sharks practically go door-to-door pitching their offense to anyone who might take it up.

Have you ever met a person like that?

In the early days of ministry, Gary and I discovered there was a small group of people from our church that was meeting every week to gossip about us under the guise of prayer. Before we knew about this, we had hired the leader of this group to do electrical work when we were building our house. Unbeknownst to us, as soon as he arrived, he was offended by the size of the house we were building. So, he called a prayer meeting to discuss it. He later called Gary and told him his opinion on the matter, and that there was a group covering the issue in prayer. Oh boy! This is a classic example of how sharks maneuver to find other sharks. This is also a great example of how cunning sharks can be! A shark will never come right out and admit they are doing something malicious. They will always disguise gossip and slander under a positive front. In this case, when my husband told the man that the church was not paying us a dime and we were paying for our house out of our business income, he suddenly grew quiet. Then after a long pause, he said, "Well I suppose the church should be paying you something." My husband never heard from him again and, I might add, he never worked on our house again either.

That's an extreme situation, but all of us can easily fall into the trap of passing our offenses on to others, or going sideways with a problem instead of directly to the source.

Do you want to know why we often find ourselves in trouble with people?

We don't do what the Bible says—we don't go to the person that we have an issue with. What would happen if we opened the lines of communication with people and just said, "When you said that, I felt like you didn't care about our friendship. What did you mean by that?" Too often, we go to sources we know will agree with our opinions and take up our offenses. We repeat the story, and when they make a comment like "I can't believe she said that," we feel justified. Sometimes, we can even go from being slightly upset about a situation to harboring full-blown anger at somebody simply because of the prodding of others.

"If I were you, I would have…"

"After all you've done for her? That was so wrong of her to…"

"That's so wrong; you should…"

The language of offense resonates like venom in our souls. And the worst part is we plant that same venom in everyone we spew our offenses to. When we hold unforgiveness and offense in our hearts, we take those people's sins upon ourselves.

Proverbs 29:25 says the fear of human opinion disables. Trusting God protects you from that!

ACTION ITEMS

Now that you understand the five shark maneuvers, have you ever experienced one of these in your life? Which one?

_____

_____

_____

Looking back, what would you have done differently in that situation?

_____

_____

_____

Look up Matthew 10:16. What does it say?

_____

_____

_____

I Iave you ever accidentally done one of these things to someone else? How can you make it right?

_____

_____

_____

CHAPTER EIGHT:
IS EVERYONE THAT WOUNDS A SHARK?

"We are very good lawyers for our own mistakes but very good judges for the mistakes of others."

—Anonymous

Is everyone that wounds us a shark? Certainly not!

Jesus speaks of sheep, goats, and wolves in the book of Matthew. Difficult people fall into the category of wolves and goats. Goats are stubborn, self-willed, and will eat anything—and they can do a lot of damage if allowed to! Goats can destroy, and so can those who are self-centered and demand their own way. We've all acted like goats at some point or the other, but thankfully, as we see the error of our ways and the negative outcomes, we turn to God and change our course of action by the power of His Spirit.

When Gary and I first married, I'll never forget driving into an impoverished rural town of Oklahoma to visit one of his college friends. Winding down a country drive, we came upon several dilapidated, abandoned cars, weeds peeping out from under the hoods, and vines wrapped around the side mirrors. To my surprise, the hood ornament of a rusted station wagon was a brown and white goat, standing tall and proud as if to say, "I have conquered!" It was humorous to behold as he let out an obnoxious bleat. Just when a goat thinks he's arrived, he's really standing on a heap of junk!

Sometimes it can be challenging to determine whether someone is a goat or a sheep. They both bleat! Sheep have little to no ulterior motives and don't have to get their way or focus on themselves alone. Sheep will follow leaders who care for them and rarely are caught in the middle of divisions or chewing on gossip-filled morsels. Goats, however, will stir up trouble. And wolves are altogether out to destroy and devour sheep and goats alike. The wolves will use goats to help mask their intent and carry out their hidden agendas. Both goats and wolves do not have the will of the Lord in mind.

Jesus gave us a picture of judgment in Matthew 25:31-34, 41, and 46 (NIV) where He shared,

> *When the Son of Man comes in his glory, and all the angels with him, he will sit on his glorious throne. All the nations will be gathered before him, and he will separate the people one from another as a shepherd separates the sheep from the goats. He will put the sheep on his right and the goats on his left. Then the King will say to those on his right, "Come you who are blessed by my father; take your inheritance, the kingdom prepared for you since the creation of the world." Then he will say to those on his left, "Depart from me, you who are cursed, into the eternal fire prepared for the devil and his angels." Then they will go away to eternal punishment, but the righteous to eternal life.*

Do people change or grow? Yes, they do! Lasting change and freedom only come from the power of God working in us when we invite Jesus to be Lord of our lives. His Word is the true divider between our soul and spirit, and rightfully divides truth so we can see our real selves, not the rationalized version we prefer to see. These can be revelatory moments where God opens places in wounded areas of our soul and let's us see the truth, so He can heal what has held us in captivity. We can all grow through challenging situations as we deal with relationships and people. It's always a choice. But it's certain we won't grow unless we come under the authorities God has placed in our lives that help us see the truth about ourselves and others.

Sometimes the deepest hurts we experience come from those with whom we have the strongest bonds. Disagreements or painful wounds from someone you've invested your life in can feel devastating, whether a spouse or adult child, and can even create separations that are permanent. That's not the outcome anyone wants in a relationship. I have counseled with people who have experienced the pain of divorce, and they equated their agony to an ongoing death, except instead of healing from losing a person through death, the pain continues to resurface every time their children are exchanged or they make attempts to rebuild their lives. We can see why God hates divorce, because the pain it brings affects people and children so deeply. God's love can bring restoration for your soul if not for the relationship. We may not be able to make people's decisions, but we can choose to forgive and be made whole in Him. *"For your Maker is your husband—the Lord of hosts is His name—and the Holy One of Israel is your Redeemer"* (Isaiah 54:5, AMPC).

You're Not Their Answer

I had just been through a time where it seemed I was giving and giving, coasting along with no seeming consequence of personal neglect and time. It is better to give than to receive, right? Then suddenly, from left field, a mounting barrage of attacks surfaced from various people we had tried to love and give our hearts to help. Just preceding this, we had been warned by a trusted fellow minister that people didn't need our money, but they needed to have faith in God so they could learn to receive for themselves. At the time, I thought it was strange he said this, but it struck a place in my heart. As I began to think about it and pray, I saw many times Gary and I had given financially to fix things in people's lives or situations, believing that this would answer their problems. It didn't! Those people were in trouble because of choices they were making. We removed the consequences for them, but we didn't remove the root issues! To our disbelief, these people found themselves in the same situations over and over again.

As I looked back on the many circumstances we were dealing with, I realized they were all in some way related to people's perceptions and choices concerning money. Then the Holy Spirit showed me that because Gary and I had been called to share principles about seeking and advancing God's Kingdom, and specifically in the area of money, the enemy had released an attack using the people's financial lack and wrong mind-set toward finances as a trap for our inexperience.

The blessing of the Lord and obedience to His teachings had brought our success, and we were sharing it with others, but we had assumed false responsibility for others' problems. The enemy intended to wear us out with turmoil involving people who chronically made bad decisions with their finances and who were unwilling to follow the teaching. Yet we somehow felt responsible for their lives and to "fix" their issues. The enemy wanted us to get hurt, hardened, and to think that God had not been faithful.

On a tough day where I felt like I was carrying the weight of problems from all directions, God said to me, "Have I let you down?" As I thought about it, I said, "No, you never have, but people have!" It hit me. I was beginning to get a religious mind-set that God was making me go through all of this turmoil when, in fact, He had nothing to do with it! I was taking it on myself because people were making me feel like it was my responsibility. Or was it me who made me feel this way?

What I learned could save you a tremendous amount of trouble! Listen carefully because it could keep you from becoming wounded and bitter. You are not someone's answer. You are an example of what the answer can do in someone's life, and you are compelled to share how you did it by God's Word and His grace, but only their yielding in obedience to God is their answer. Let me say it again, "Obedience to God and His Word are their answer. You can never do for someone what they are not willing to do for themselves.

Hurting people hurt people. We've heard it so many times! When people see how the Lord blesses your obedience and honors your life, it will bring others to a decision: to either rejoice that there are answers from God they can emulate or to become jealous at what they will not choose. This is between them and God. You can pray. You can instruct and preach. You can love, but you cannot possess the land for another. Can you imagine how Joshua felt when he and Caleb went into the promised land of God and had to leave all of those negative spies and people in the wilderness who started the journey with them but would not finish with God? If we will not, God cannot. The question remains, "Will you allow someone's disobedience to cause you to doubt God's goodness?" The blessing of the Lord brings wealth, but He adds no sorrow to it.

We must be compassionate but not enable people to blame or shame us out of God's blessings. Compassion says, "I understand what you are going through is not easy. Here's the answer. It's not silver or gold, but the healing power of God and His Words of life that will change everything." We have tithed, sown, worked diligently, and given in obedience to God's Word. It brings blessing! We have learned that fixing someone's issues for them only delays the inevitable. God, Himself set a system of sowing and reaping in the earth to bless *and* correct us all. When we realize what we are sowing is not producing a good harvest, we must make changes. If you step in and "fix" everything for another person, then you are reaping the consequences of others' choices and behaviors. What reason would they have to change anything? What will the outcome be for you?

No one can steal our peace or joy from us unless we allow it. We are responsible for our lives, our decisions, and our choices. I had to analyze why I was always trying to "fix" things to my own harm. When you step into enabling or taking false responsibility, eventually, you break down emotionally and physically. These are questions I had to ask myself, and I encourage you to do the same.

- Who is responsible for the issue? (responsibility)

- Who has the authority to ultimately solve the problem? (authority)

- How am I hindering their change? (accountability)

- What is my motive for helping? (motive)

When I asked myself these questions, I realized much of my life had been spent taking false responsibility for solving problems that I did not have the God-given authority to fix. Was I doing this because I wanted to be loved, admired, or appreciated? Was I getting my identity from performing or from the Lord Jesus Christ? How many times had this controlled my life, my joy, my peace? All of the times I had cried myself to sleep because someone I had helped had stuck a dagger in my back were due to a lack of understanding of where my responsibility started and stopped. I recognized that love deficits in my own heart had caused me to perform for love instead of just obeying God. How many times had I neglected my responsibility to God, myself, or my family while trying to be superwoman to others? How many times had I gotten in the way of someone making real change happen in their lives because I thought that "good Christians" who were successful were obligated to fix everyone's problems? How many times had I caused people I loved to not reap the consequences of a life-changing lesson because I played their savior instead of letting Jesus assume that role in their lives? Ouch!

Sometimes my motives were right but my choice was wrong. And sometimes my motives were wrong—to get something someone couldn't give me, self-worth. God has healed many wounds in my heart and restored places that were devastated by goats, wolves... and sharks! I have had to learn that I must be at the command of the Lord, not the dictates of people, pressures, or my own issues. If you are giving to a shark, look out! You are casting your pearls... to be trampled and eaten.

So often in life, the bites we receive are from someone who has been bitten. We have all bitten others ourselves! I think of the lyrics by Art Garfunkel: "I bruise you. You bruise me. We all bruise so easily." Misunderstandings and the lack of empathy for what another person is dealing with may be the biggest contributors to relationship rifts and difficult situations. I constantly hear from disillusioned leaders and heartbroken pastors who are ready to quit because someone they have loved or invested in has wounded or left them. I encourage them not to abort the mission because of a lost friend or team member. Although some relationships will not be repaired, there are encouraging stories of restoration when we choose to grow and stay the course. Trust can be broken, but it also has the potential to be rebuilt as the amazing story I now share verifies.

I hung up the phone and fell to my knees sobbing and begging for God's forgiveness. This was the third attempt I had made to fix a relationship that I knew was not going in a good direction. I deeply loved this family; they were there from the beginning of our ministry. I didn't know just how much my own insecurity had relied on them being by our side until the relationship was shaken and they had pulled away. I was willing to do anything to fix it. I guess I knew in my heart that wasn't the real answer, but I didn't think I could handle the alternative of them leaving our life. I was afraid so I caved. When I couldn't reach them, I left a message on their answering machine that I was so sorry for anything we may have done to hurt them, to please forgive us if we had… that we wanted to please them, but we "had to obey God." I had no more uttered these words than the conviction of God hit me like a ton of bricks. I apologized for having to obey God, trying to please them and do what I thought would maintain the relationship? It was true. Subtly, I had begun to perform for them to keep peace at the expense of my relationship with God. This was my responsibility, not theirs. Now, I was broken, feeling I had let God down too.

Eventually, the relationship deteriorated, the wounds went deep, partially because I loved them so much and partially because I had allowed the priority of the friendship to be out of line spiritually, motivated by my fear of losing them. I repented to God for our part of the fracture that caused the split, and I released to Him the wounds I felt were inflicted on us. Years went by, and at times I mourned the loss but kept on with the vision. A wise woman once told me that people would come and go but to stick with the vision and it would grow. As hard as that seemed, it was true and meant that I had to keep my allegiance to God and His vision as my first priority.

One Sunday morning, seven years later, I spotted the couple in our worship service. They were back. My heart was clean and clear, and

I knew there was no longer pain or any blockage toward them. I felt love but wondered what they felt or what brought them back that day. They continued to come back week after week and then requested a meeting with us, which we gladly accepted. I have encouraged many leaders on the brink of quitting with the story of what happened in our meeting that day.

As we sat together, I'm sure both of us feeling some apprehension and relief, they shared a heartfelt apology for the way they had treated us and asked for our forgiveness. It was real, and I could feel their genuine pain and remorse. My husband and I listened as our estranged friends asked what they could do to return to church and restore the relationship. We immediately began to take responsibility and apologize for our part in the misunderstanding, but before we could finish, she stopped us and said, "No, the Lord showed me it wasn't you, it was us; we were acting like spoiled brats." With her strong words of conviction and her willingness to take full responsibility (even though I knew we had been far from perfect leaders), I saw authentic, sincere repentance. It set my heart at ease, and the love I had for them grew even more that day. It had never left. Since our parting, they shared with us their difficult journey through several churches and jobs, and the painful impact on their children. My eyes filled with tears and my heart with compassion for them and all they had been through. I would never have wanted them or anyone to suffer in this way! I've seen this suffering in too many lives, and it's the reason to tell this story. We hugged and prayed. After seven years, it felt like a long-lost dream to see our fellowship restored. In time, they once again became a very important part of the ministry and are impacting the world for God today.

When we stop controlling or taking false responsibility for people's decisions, they are free to decide, and the Holy Spirit can work in our hearts to keep priorities straight. Honestly, we could not have followed God's plan while trying to please someone above Him. This is always the temptation when we want people to join our cause or stay in a relationship. I am stronger today because I had to choose. They are stronger because of their choice. I learned about myself and had to turn over the weakness in my soul to allow God to grow me into a woman He can trust. The Scripture says, *"Whose weakness was turned to strength."* God's love suffers long, and He is patient with all of us. If we allow Him, He will turn our weakness around and make us strong in Him.

Is everyone who bites a shark? No. They've possibly been bitten by sharks themselves and may mistake you for the predator! There is restoration in Christ, but each person has to want it sincerely enough to be humble before God, seek the truth, and accept personal responsibility. Rarely are any of us 100 percent right or wrong. It's often the area in between that causes breakdowns. If we can't have empathy for others or communicate honestly, real relationship cannot exist. How many enterprises, churches, and lives have been impacted by, as my friend said, "spoiled brat" attitudes? We all get them, but if we want to advance, we must change to grow and impact God's Kingdom. James says, "Why do quarrels happen among you? You want something and don't get it. You fight, you argue. You have not because you don't ask God. And when you do, you ask amiss to consume it on your own lust." Before any of us write off others as sharks, let's examine our own hearts and responsibility. God is looking for fruit in our lives and integrity in our hearts. That is always our responsibility.

There is hope and healing in God and His affirming love! We may not forget the pain inflicted by life, by our mistakes, or by a goat or wolf (sharks), but we can be resolved of feeling its sting in our lives. Even death itself has been swallowed up by the sacrifice of Jesus! "*'For I know the plans I have for you,' declares the Lord, 'plans to prosper you, and not to harm you, plans to give you hope and a future'*" (Jeremiah 29:11, NIV).

ACTION ITEMS

Have you ever falsely judged somebody and later discovered you were wrong? How did that make you or the other person feel?

_____

_____

_____

Read Romans 2:1. What does this verse mean to you?

_____

_____

_____

Look up Matthew 7:1. What does it say?

_____

_____

_____

What should you do when you are tempted to cast judgment on somebody else?

_____

_____

_____

CHAPTER NINE:
WOUNDED BY SHARKS

"There is only one way to avoid criticism: do nothing, say nothing, and be nothing."

–Aristotle

"My problem is with you!" they said, as they pointed their finger at me. The stinging words cut through my heart like a laser. I had prayerfully called this meeting to express our love and appreciation and to repair any breach between a group of people that I cared about more than any other. Now the focus was on me and my shortcomings. As if being sentenced in a court of law, I couldn't forget the words that echoed in my mind. I had spent my life devoted to the well-being of these young adults. I had chosen to forgo many personal wants and spend almost every waking hour (and some nights) for 35 years for these, my children. I didn't regret it, but in this debilitating moment, I felt completely unappreciated, even attacked. Every insecurity I had fought much of my life tried to resurface and drown me. Now it seemed many of them, or maybe all of them, had serious hurts toward me. What had happened? How did we get here? Brokenness is all I felt.

For days, I tried to forget the looks and words of hurt that attempted to smother me. Negative childhood patterns tried to regain control of my thoughts. Self-defeating words wreaked havoc on my sleep. It didn't help that I was jet-lagged and emotionally exhausted from trying to fix problems all over the place. I felt like I had tried my best and had fallen seriously short. This was different than any conflict with a person I had ever experienced. In other conflicts, I could argue my case, but in this, I cared so much for them that all I could feel was painful remorse. I tried to express my commitment and even a laundry list of actions proving my love. Then I realized how *they* were hurting. They had tried to be strong and do their best to handle ministry problems for us but had not shared their personal mounting hurts and issues. Our lack of knowledge of their hurts created a lack of empathy on my part. I didn't know how difficult things had been. I only knew the overwhelming pressures I felt, and since they managed many of these areas, we naturally turned to them to take responsibility to solve the issues. We were all in pain, truth be told. And at least on some days, we were all performing for love and acceptance.

When we are in pain, it's only human nature to blame someone. I knew this. During years of counseling families, it was always the parent who offered security to the kids that got the blunt of their children's criticism and pain when the irresponsible parent walked out. Their hurt was so great it had to be vented. It had to go somewhere. They blamed the person who appeared strong enough to handle it or who cared enough they wouldn't reject them and leave. The temptation to blame loomed over each person, including me.

We were all over our heads in a sea of demands and personal anchors of inadequacy. What I was struggling to navigate, so were they. As things unfolded, I could see their personal pain; dealing with difficult people was overriding our relationships. In their suffering, I may have appeared to not care, but the fact was I didn't know. They couldn't do much about the hurtful people who had stuck daggers in their hearts or the people who criticized or laid traps to ensnare them. As leaders and parents, we were their only safe house… or were we? I didn't want to be another person wielding a dagger. I knew I had to decide. My response to their pain was of paramount importance. If I retreated in agony and put up walls, as I had in other painful situations, all could be lost. As rocky or difficult as it seemed, the wound had been opened, and now healing could happen if I could get my eyes off of my feelings and onto understanding. I had to take personal responsibility for my contribution to the problem.

Emotional hurts are like cancers of the soul. If we don't get them out, they can poison the whole soul and body. We all avoid the surgery, but it's better to extract the cancer and return to a healthy place. Through open heartfelt communication and tears, we started mending fences and heard each other. Everyone says things they don't mean in a moment of hurt. Talking and listening with empathy led to a path of reestablishing everyone's commitment to one another and strengthened family bonds. There was no lack of love on anyone's part, only a lack of understanding.

Identifying the "Why"

It's important to know why someone may be acting in a way that is hurtful. If a person is hurting, they will most likely take that hurt somewhere. Families are that place where we often release our hurts and sort through life's tough problems. I am not perfect and neither is my family, but we are family. Families must work through the troubles and hurts they feel to find the answers and relationships they desperately need. We were all affected by the same shark attacks. Most revolved around chronically problematic, people-related issues, but at the root of all of the hurt was a thief named Satan who tried to distort our love, separate us from communication, and entice us to believe lies, to accuse and blame each other. He is the accuser of the brethren and the father of lies.

These are never one-time cures. When our children were at home, the first three days of family vacations were often tumultuous because we had all been busy and disconnected. It always took several days to break down walls of division and prioritize our lives. Hurts were mended, and by the end of the week, we were having the time of our lives, laughing and bonding over a campfire or a hike. I always hated to return to the normal pressures of life because I knew, once again, schedules, people issues, pressures, and rifts would try to divide us. How much more do we need to create opportunities to get understanding when adult pressures abound? Relationships are delicate, and words can never be retracted, but by God's healing, they can be redacted.

I started thinking about basketball or football teams and how each player has a position for which they are most gifted. Comparing one's strengths in their position to another's weaknesses in that area isn't fair to anyone. It takes a team to accomplish the win. It also takes a coach who knows how to bring out the best in each member and deal with attitudes that surface when the going gets rough. I had been a coach cheering, sacrificing, and believing for my family to win, but at the same time, I had modeled a life of saying yes to demands and even shark attacks that resulted in "bites from my time" and me saying no to the ones I loved. Every yes in your life will cost you something. If you don't draw borders around what is important to you, Satan will take advantage of those you hold dear. Everyone must make the personal choice to say no to distractions and to wholeheartedly serve and follow God. Jesus said, "Let your yes be yes and your no be no." What you say yes or no to will determine your destiny.

Are there times to say no to family? Yes, if it interferes with God's plan. Some families try to control through manipulation and guilt. It's certainly normal to have influence with the people we love and to help them see the consequences of decisions and allegiances, but it is altogether different to use or abuse family members through control. Again, the enemy will attempt to enter into relationships to control by using a familiar voice that we don't always recognize as a shark. Jesus had to rebuke Peter when Peter fallaciously tried to influence Him to abandon His calling. Each of us will have to decide to follow Jesus for ourselves. This is the great division. *"Do not suppose that I came to bring peace on earth. I did not come to bring peace, but a sword. For I have come to set a man against his father, a daughter against her mother, and a daughter-in-law against her mother-in-law"* (Matthew 10:34-35, NIV).

There cannot be true peace while sin and disobedience to God exist on the earth. Zechariah 9:9-10 (NKJV) say, *"Behold your King is coming to you. He is just and having salvation... He shall speak peace to the nations; His dominion shall be from sea to sea."* Isaiah 48:22 (NIV) clarifies, *"'There is no peace,' says the Lord, 'for the wicked.'"*

Yet when we agree that God's Word is the truth and have common goals, this doesn't guarantee there will not be disagreements or misunderstandings. And just as in Peter's case, we can say we love but get it wrong when it comes to attitudes or our influence. Jesus's rebuke of Peter left him with two choices: Offense leading to betrayal or to receive His leadership and make the changes. Even though Peter later denied Him, Jesus confronted him after His resurrection to ask him, "Peter, do you love me?" Jesus asked three times. Peter reaffirmed his love three times, one for every denial. Each time, Jesus commissioned Peter to feed His sheep and lambs.

When Jesus's own mother and brothers showed up to see Him while He was ministering in a nearby town, their motive may have been to help Him, but their direction and communication were way off. We can see in prior verses that they thought He was beside Himself—in other words, a lunatic! When they asked to see Him to interrupt His ministry, Jesus responded with, "Who are my mother and brothers? Those who do the will of God." I used to think those were strong words to say to your mother, but given the context, He was modeling for us that even family can get in the way of following God's will. Our first allegiance must always be to God. The rich, young ruler was confronted with a decision on whether or not to follow Jesus. He felt the cost was too great, and he chose to honor himself instead of God. The cost to obey God is not too great, but the cost of letting sharks attack you and the ones you love can be fatal if not detected and dealt with quickly.

One minister shared with me he had seen more ministry families dissolve recently than at any time in his life. The spirit of witchcraft driven by satanic sharks has consumed the nations and there is an all-out war to destroy families, and anything righteous, especially families that stand for God's Word. U.S. families dissolve at a greater rate than any other industrialized nation, and we lead the world in the number of fathers absent from the home. Additionally, we perform more abortions per capita and have the most permissible divorce laws in the world. The battle lines are drawn, and everything hidden is being exposed on all fronts. These issues have been underlying and undermining the nation's foundation for decades. The brainwashing of men and women through media and celebrity icons tore down our foundations, and they now attempt to demand law and order be abolished for their set of unrighteous demands. We do not wrestle with flesh and blood but with powers that are unseen in heavenly realms. These are the real sharks that play evil games with the lives of those who fall prey to them. The Scripture calls them principalities, might, and dominion. Our first allegiance must be to God and then our family and calling.

Finding Resolution

Problems will occur in any endeavor, including families. It's how we solve the issues we face that gives all relationships meaning.

M. Scott Peck said in *The Road Less Traveled*:

"It is in the whole process of meeting and solving problems that life has meaning. Problems are the cutting edge that distinguishes between success and failure. Problems call forth courage and wisdom. It is only because of problems that we grow mentally and spiritually… It is through the pain of confronting and resolving problems that we learn."

As Benjamin Franklin said, "Those things that hurt, instruct."

Learning to attack the real problems and not the person keeps our focus and helps alleviate defensiveness. In problem solving, we must know the facts and be slow to rush to judgment. We think we understand what's happened, but often we are wrong or have a faulty opinion of what happened. This requires patience and an investment of time. Ask questions to understand, not point a finger. Listing the various options to resolve the problem eliminates the emotional triggers that can set off personal attacks. If things get personal, then it may require a time to cool off and pray before re-engaging the issues. Oftentimes, there are past issues or unresolved conflicts at the root of these types of encounters. Finally, choose the best solution. Keep a positive outlook, and recognize that even hard situations have a positive side to them. If a wound is under the surface, bringing it to the light can be the first step to healing. Every conversation must have a healthy dose of love. You may not be able to retain a working relationship with a family member, but you can retain a family relationship and choose to not withhold love regardless of a disagreement. Find at least one thing to agree on, and let that be mutual love and respect.

We have found that media is most often the enemy of not only time but also communication. How much eyeball time you give the important people in your life will determine the quality of the relationships. It's interesting that in a world where everyone is "our friend" on social media, we have diminished the tight bonds with people who should truly be our friends and allies. These social pseudo-friendships undermine true intimacy. Hide the cell phone, and reclaim conversation as your number one tool to protect your family, your enterprise, and your ministry.

Time and appreciation for one another and handling crises in a positive way are the real keys to communicating for understanding. Recognize the real sharks!

I want to close this chapter with this encouragement from Mother Teresa:

> *People are often unreasonable, irrational, and self-centered. Forgive them anyway.*
>
> *If you are kind, people may accuse you of selfish, ulterior motives. Be kind anyway.*
>
> *If you are successful, you will win some unfaithful friends and some genuine enemies. Succeed anyway.*
>
> *If you are honest and sincere, people may deceive you. Be honest and sincere anyway.*
>
> *What you spend years creating, others could destroy overnight. Create anyway.*

If you find serenity and happiness, some may be jealous. Be happy anyway.

The good you do today will often be forgotten. Do good anyway.

Give the best you have, and it may never be enough. Give your best anyway.

In the final analysis, it is between you and God. It was never between you and them anyway.

ACTION ITEMS

Who do you need to resolve a conflict with today?

_____

_____

_____

Are there emotional hurts and painful words people have spoken against you that you need to let go of? Second Corinthians 2:5-8 say to forgive so people aren't "overwhelmed by excessive sorrow." Luke 6:37 tells us to forgive so <u>we</u> can be forgiven. How are you going to deal with these emotional wounds?

_____

_____

_____

_____

_____

CHAPTER TEN:
THE SHARK CURE

When you see a big wave coming toward you in the ocean, do you just stand there and get clobbered, or do you turn around and ride it?

Sharks will come in life, but they don't have to deter us from our destinies. In fact, when we submit these situations to God and handle them His way, they can end up preparing and opening doors for our future. Just because you face opposition doesn't mean you have to be overcome by it. Goliath was a big shark in the Bible, but with God's help, facing Goliath is what opened the door for David's promotion! Trust that you are safe and well cared for by a Father who loves you and wants to see you having fun as you live a life for Him. Romans 8:28 (NIV) says, *"And we know that in all things God works for the good of those who love him, who have been called according to his purpose."* This admonition isn't suggesting that God brought the issue, but when we pray in His Spirit as referenced earlier in the chapter, we know that God takes even the difficulties of life and turns them around to promote us for our good!

The Bible is equipped with remedies and lines of defense against sharks! Let's take a look at Psalm 37 and some of the powerful tactics

God gives us to fend against shark attacks:

1. Don't fret.

Know any champion worriers? I have to admit I used to be one! From worrying about our children to worrying about our finances, I would stay up at night worrying about everything! Sound familiar? Well, I know from experience that not only is worry a surefire way to have permanent circles under your eyes, but it also leads to much more serious dangers. Psalm 37:8-9 (NIV) tell us, *"Refrain from anger and turn from wrath; do not fret—it leads only to **evil**. For those who are evil will be destroyed, but those who hope in the Lord will inherit the land."*

When we worry and fret over everything, we don't make right decisions. That's why it is so important to get your mind right and align yourself with God's Word when sharks appear.

So how do we have a peaceful attitude while swimming in shark-infested waters? I know it sounds impossible! Are you picturing scenes from *Jaws* right now?

I want you to know IT IS absolutely possible to be completely protected when surrounded by danger and evil. Pray instead of worrying!

Years ago, I was asked to speak to a large group of women at a women's meeting. Well, anyone who knows me knows that I'm high energy. So I'm bouncing around the stage, waving my arms around as I'm talking to these women, and you know what? You could've heard a pin drop! These women wanted nothing to do with me or what I had to say. Ouch! I'm not going to lie; that hurt!

But guess what? Instead of running off the stage with my tail between my legs, I saw a fork in the road. You know that famous poem that talks about the road less traveled? Well, I saw my road: disappointment, anger, and defeat OR forgiveness, courage, and faith.

In the culture, anger and unforgiveness are the "norm," but I want to encourage you to take the road less traveled, just like I did in that situation.

I stopped my talk, and I just called out to the Holy Spirit to fill that room and fill those hearts, and He did! It was a different room after I was done praying. The heaviness was gone, and those hearts were open! Years before that, I wouldn't have had the courage to do that, but once I knew WHO I was in Christ, and believed in Him for every victory, these situations didn't break me down. They became opportunities to make my faith EVEN STRONGER!

The enemy will try to convince you that the battle is lost before it even begins! Don't buy into it! In fact, in my experience, your breakthrough is usually right on the other side of those shark-infested waters.

2. Trust the Lord.

When she was a child, my daughter Amy suffered from very intense night terrors after we had been in a car wreck. It made for sleepless nights for both of us. If you are a parent, I don't have to tell you that there is nothing more gut-wrenching in the world than seeing your child suffer. To make matters worse, during this same time period, my husband, Gary, was suffering from terrible panic attacks. I knew our whole family was under attack!

Ever feel like nothing is working out? Like the enemy is throwing everything but the kitchen sink at you and your family?

Maybe a coworker is speaking lies about you, or you're tangled up in a huge financial burden that seems hopeless, or maybe you are dealing with jealousy and manipulation from fair-weather friends when you start succeeding.

Been there! Done ALL of that!

The enemy is going to use people or situations to come against you; he is going to try to keep you from all God has for you.

Do you know when things turned around for Amy, for Gary, and for our whole family? When we made the choice to stand firm, pray for God to infuse His power into our circumstances, and trust that He had already granted us the victory. It was only a short time later we answered the calling to pastor and realized that the warfare was intended to thwart our destiny.

Philippians 4:6 (NIV) tells us, *"Do not be anxious about anything, but in every situation, by prayer and petition, with thanksgiving, present your requests to God."*

Your happiness, your success, your peace, EVERYTHING depends on your decision to trust in God. When you do that, the sharks in your life no longer have power over you. When you do that, the enemy has to flee!

Worrying is just us trying to be God's backseat driver. *Be careful, God. Look out for that, God. Isn't this a faster, safer way, God?* Ha! God created you. He knows you better than anyone. He knows where you are going, and He knows exactly how to get you there. But you can't "get there" and excel in your God-given assignment if you are constantly doubting, questioning, and worrying about the outcome.

You are only truly safe when you put God in the driver's seat. Don't be a backseat driver; just enjoy the company, and trust that He will deliver you to your destination safely.

3. Do good.

Love your enemies. Love your enemies. Love your enemies.

No matter how many times you tell yourself this important advice, sometimes it just seems impossible! So how do we really love people who treat us badly? How do we not have feelings of anger and resentment when people do wrong to us, spread lies about us, or just flat-out try to trip us up?

The simple answer: we don't.

Do I have your attention now? We don't; the Holy Spirit does!

When the sharks are biting at you, and your flesh reacts with anger and unforgiveness, you need to call on the Holy Spirit and ask Him to infuse God's love into your heart. Don't fall into the trap of sin when evildoers mount attacks against you. Your destiny is too important!

Psalm 37.27-28 (ESV) tell us, *"Turn away from evil and do good; so shall you dwell forever. For the Lord loves justice; he will not forsake his saints."*

When you give way to anger and resentment, you lose so much more than a moment or a day; you take your focus off of your assignment. Our God is a just and loving God. No matter how many sharks are around you, no matter how sharp their words, keep your cool, keep your eyes on God, and remember His promises. He will protect you and grant you the desires of your heart.

4. Enjoy and delight in the Lord.

Psalm 37:4-5 (NIV) tell us, *"Take delight in the Lord, and he will give you the desires of your heart. Commit your way to the Lord; trust in him and he will do this."*

I always think of Martha and Mary when I read this Bible verse. Martha is busy in the kitchen and annoyed with her sister Mary, who is sitting "lazily" at the feet of Jesus. Do you ever feel like Martha? Overscheduled, overworked, overburdened? Unfortunately, I think this is most people.

It's "normal" to be overly busy in the culture, but that kind of lifestyle comes at a high price.

Your ability to rise above the sharks, those people who want to drag you down with untruths, drama, or manipulation, depends on you taking the focus OFF of the sharks and putting your time, energy, and heart back where it belongs—in God's capable hands.

Psalm 37:23-24 (NIV) tell us, *"The Lord makes firm the steps of the one who delights in him; though he may stumble, he will not fall, for the Lord upholds him with his hand."*

I'm sure you've seen movies where the character is high above the ground and the best friend whispers, *"Don't look down."* Without fail, the character looks down and nearly falls. When we look away from God, our focus is back on the danger, the sharks, those who want to see us fall. I want to encourage you to not look away from God, even for a second! Make time every day to get into His presence and hear His will for your life.

You see, when every minute is scheduled, it is that much harder for the Holy Spirit to move spontaneously in our lives! All the hustle and bustle makes it even harder to make out that still, small voice.

God is always trying to speak to us. He has so much to tell us. When we sit still at the feet of Jesus, like Mary did, we are truly doing what God made us to do: love Him and delight in Him.

When we get in His presence and delight in Him, we are opening up the lines of communication. We are allowing Him to move in our hearts and in our lives. God is nothing if not personal, and if it doesn't feel that way, you might need a little less Martha and a little more Mary in your life.

The best antidote for overcoming the sharks in your life is to fix your eyes on God, keep your focus on His Word, and get into His amazing presence daily.

5. Commit.

Commitment is certainly not the hip thing in the culture right now. Roughly 50 percent of marriages end in divorce!

Did you know that your commitment level in one area is your commitment level in ALL areas? Luke 16:10 (NIV) says, *"Whoever can be trusted with very little can also be trusted with much, and whoever is dishonest with very little will also be dishonest with much."* No matter how many sharks you are facing and how scary they might appear, your commitment to God should not ebb and flow, because true commitment in ALL things is a steady, everyday choice.

Psalm 37:5-6 (ESV) tell us, *"Commit your way to the Lord; trust in him, and he will act. He will bring forth your righteousness as the light, and your justice as the noonday."*

In difficult seasons of life, when it seems like there are far more sharks than allies, it is YOUR commitment to God, YOUR commitment to righteousness, that will enable God to move in YOUR life and help you overcome any circumstance. God needs YOUR commitment to protect you and to grant you the victory. He cannot bless you the way He wants to unless you trust and commit to Him in ALL things.

There are going to be days when you just don't feel like it, when you are dog-tired and feel like giving up, but when you learn to rely on His strength, His wisdom, and His power, evildoers will have no power over you.

So often we feel like God has abandoned us to our fate, that He doesn't see our struggle or care about our pain. But guess what? Many times when you feel like you are waiting for God to act, He is waiting on YOU to commit.

Give 100 percent commitment to God, and He will return that and so much more.

6. Refrain from anger.

One of the quickest ways to miss out on ALL God has for you—and He has so much—is to get angry at the sharks in your life when they attack.

Years ago, Kirsten and I went to Japan for a girls' trip. On the last day, as we were leaving our hotel and taking our bags out to the line of taxis, we got assigned to a very rude driver. Of course, right?! Everything seems to be going so smoothly, until, all of a sudden, it's not.

He tried to fit our bags in the trunk, but when he couldn't get them to fit, he became angry with us; and he got even angrier when we told him they would fit if he just tried it a different way. He didn't like that, so he yelled at us to get out!

If there was ever a moment to be angry, it was this one! It had been such a perfect trip up until that moment. The enemy was swooping in and trying to steal our joy with this over-the-top nonsense. This driver got angrier and angrier because he refused to be patient, listen to us, and try it another way.

Have you ever experienced this? You know the way to make it work, but the sharks in your life have zero interest in hearing it, and when their way doesn't work, somehow it's *your* fault. It's so frustrating!

Years ago, I would've fallen into that trap. *"He should've listened to us; He should've been more patient."* Don't let someone else's *shoulda* moments become yours.

Ever notice that sharks have a habit of trying to muck things up right when you are feeling great? That's not an accident. Sharks don't attack just to steal a moment; they come to steal God's promises from your heart and put you on the path that they are on, a path of anger, doubt, and manipulation.

In that moment, I chose to stay calm. I chose to let that man's anger remain *his* anger, not mine. I chose to show my daughter that YOU CAN overcome even the most frustrating situations with the peace of the Holy Spirit.

And you know what? We found a driver who listened to us and got the bags to fit, and I gave him a huge tip! Ha! You see, when you reach for anger, you miss out on opportunities for God to bless you, and he has so many blessings in store for you.

7. Inherit His promises.

Part of receiving God's blessings and inheriting His promises depends on your choice to reach for righteousness when you are facing evildoers, people who want to knock you off of God's path.

The sharks are going to seem bigger than they actually are. Don't break a sweat. You've got this! YOU CAN overcome the problems by keeping your eyes on God's promises.

Psalm 37:28-29 (NIV) tell us "*Wrongdoers will be completely destroyed; the offspring of the wicked will perish. The righteous will inherit the land and dwell in it forever.*"

You are a child of God; you have been given an amazing inheritance. Don't throw it away by letting the sharks convince you that they have the victory.

I once heard a great saying: "*No one can make you feel inferior without your consent.*"

I love that! In the culture, we are taught to tiptoe around, always anxious about unknowingly slighting someone. But life isn't perfect, and we can't depend on everyone to speak loving words at all times.

There are always going to be evildoers who speak words of manipulation and negativity, and your feelings are going to be all over the place if you allow someone else to control them.

YOU are in control of your own feelings. When you know WHO you are and what you've been promised, you aren't swayed by the sharks when they speak lies. Instead, you will have the victory in ANY situation.

8. Speak wisdom.

Your mouth is a rudder for your life. Let me say that one more time: Your mouth is a rudder for your life!

Every direction you take is determined by what you are speaking into your environment. The cure for the sharks in your life is to stay aligned with God's Word; speak it constantly. Put verses like these up on the walls, or anywhere you will see them every day:

Psalm 37:30-31 (NIV) tell us, *"The mouths of the righteous utter wisdom, and their tongues speak what is just. The law of their God is in their hearts; their feet do not slip."*

Proverbs 18:21 (NIV) tells us, *"The tongue has the power of life and death, and those who love it will eat its fruit."*

Hebrews 4:12 tells (NIV) us, *"For the word of God is alive and active. Sharper than any double-edged sword, it penetrates even to dividing soul and spirit, joints and marrow; it judges the thoughts and attitudes of the heart."*

The sharks in your life are going to speak against the truth, against God's Word. They thrive on speaking doubt, fear, and lies. When you spend time in God's presence and get to know His Word well, His truth is stored safely inside your heart, and the naysayers, doubters, and manipulators will not be able to take it from you.

Whatever situation you are facing, ask God to infuse His power into your circumstances. He wants you to live a happy, healthy life. He wants to bless you and see you prosper. Keep your eyes on Him, and speak His Word against situations when people come against you. When you allow God to work in the situation, you win the battle over your thoughts and words. Only then can you succeed in your God-given assignment!

9. Hope in God.

When you are in the middle of shark-infested waters, it can be really hard to hold on to hope. Gary and I have spent many years in ministry. A lot of people think because we are working for God, we just sit around and read the Bible to each other, feed each other grapes, and fan each other with palm leaves. If only!

Ministry is the thing the enemy is going to try to destroy the most! We have had to deal with various sharks and people who didn't have our best interests at heart. We've had to deal with people we thought were friends but who were not happy about our success.

Know this: the bigger the calling, the bigger the enemy's attacks. I want you to know, if you feel like you are trying to walk out God's purpose and the enemy is sending shark after shark into your life, you are right! The enemy doesn't want you to succeed in your purpose; he wants to knock you off course. He is going to send lie after lie: *"This is impossible! You're going to fail! You aren't capable of greatness. You are weak."*

Have you ever heard any of these? I know I have. These obstacles always appear when I am about to have a breakthrough. Holding on to hope is the key to casting down negative thoughts. Once you lose hope, the enemy has a foothold. Don't give up! Stay the course!

Psalm 37:34 (NIV) tells us, *"Hope in the Lord and keep his way. He will exalt you to inherit the land; when the wicked are destroyed, you will see it."*

Sometimes it might feel like the sharks are winning and prospering, but God's justice will always prevail. We just have to wait patiently for His timing.

Psalm 37:7 (ESV) tells us, *"Be still before the Lord and wait patiently for him; fret not yourself over the one who prospers in his way, over the man who carries out evil devices!"*

God is for you. He loves you, and He will protect you while you are pursuing His purpose for your life.

ACTION ITEMS

Read Psalm 37:4-5. What do these verses mean to you?

_____

_____

_____

Based on this chapter, how are you going to fend off sharks in the future?

_____

_____

_____

Look up Psalm 37:23-24. What do these verses say?

_____

_____

_____

CHAPTER ELEVEN:
DISABLING A SHARK

"Sometimes we cripple people who are capable of walking because we choose to carry them."

—Anonymous

When we were starting to pastor, a mentor who had pastored for years sat us down and told us he had a word of advice for us. I was waiting for Scriptures, anointing, and great revelations to flow, but only one powerful sentence escaped his lips. He looked us in the eyes and said, "People aren't going to like you."

"What? That's it?" I thought. *"Well, I'm going to* make *them like me!"*

If I had taken that pastor's advice to heart back then, it would have saved me a lot of heartache. That's why I wrote this book! I want to give you that same advice. Not everyone is going to like you, and that's OKAY. Obey God regardless. Love people regardless. Forgive regardless. Invest your time into the people who celebrate the call of God on your life and encourage you toward your destiny in Christ.

Here are some of the shark proof principles that Gary and I learned the hard way. I want to share them with you, so you don't have to learn them the hard way!

Add No to Your Vocabulary

My daughter Kirsten has often fondly repeated this quote from Jules Renard: "The truly free man is the one who can turn down an invitation to dinner without giving an excuse."

To be honest, that sounds like the opposite position of what I've worked from my whole life!

Why is it that one little word—*no*—can be so hard to say?

Our business mentor and friend Dave Anderson changed the way Gary and I thought of the word no forever. He said, "You may think of the word no as being a negative thing, but no can be one of the most positive and liberating words in your vocabulary!"

Powerful advice!

Saying no to manipulation, time wasters, and naysayers means you can say YES to more time, freedom, critical relationships, family, God mandates, and yes, even to your dreams! Do you see what a positive word no can be?

Even if you agree that no may be one of the most powerful words in the English language, it still doesn't make it any easier to say. So how can we learn to say no to sharks? We need to know what our yes is. When we know what our yes is, we know what our no has to be!

Recently, my family was going through the *Boundaries: When to Say Yes, How to Say No to Take Control of Your Life* curriculum, and they discussed the "Reaping and Sowing" principle. "You don't want to reap what somebody else sowed," Drs. Henry Cloud and John Townsend explained. I didn't understand yet, but they had my attention. I've heard about sowing and reaping nearly all of my life—but this sounded different than anything I had ever heard before. Drs. Cloud and Townsend went on to say that if somebody else has sown bad decision after bad decision in their life, you don't want to take their consequences on yourself and reap what *they* sowed. In the meantime, they're reaping what you sowed! That's how unhealthy, codependent relationships are formed. Consequences are what teach us to make different decisions in the future. When we remove the consequences for people, they get to reap the reward of what we've sown; and we reap their consequences. We are actually *rewarding them* for bad decisions!

In this curriculum, they give the example of parents who came to them many years back. They said their son was out of control and had a problem—he wasn't taking any responsibility for his life. He was out skiing in Colorado, having fun, and he had already flunked out of multiple schools and wasn't working a job. They asked these parents, "Well, where is he living? How is he paying for his house?"

The parents told them they were paying for his housing in Colorado.

As they discussed it further, the doctor looked at them softly and said, "Your son doesn't have a problem, *you* do. You've taken all of your son's problems away for him."

When we reap what somebody else has sowed, we keep them from growing spiritually. Not only that, but also in the long run of fixing, fixing, fixing everything for everybody else, we start to grow bitter!

We think, "*I'm putting in all of the work, and they're reaping the reward! How is this fair?*" It's not! So why are you allowing it?

Verbalize Your Needs, and Set Boundaries

"You are not required to set yourself on fire to keep people warm."

—Anonymous

When a person struggles to practice self-care, one of the first things they put on the back burner is communicating their needs to the people around them. You have to be the one to draw boundaries around your life and time—nobody can do it for you! This may be as simple as asking your spouse to clean up after themselves, or it could mean having a more in-depth conversation about the changes you need to be at your best.

Your needs are important, and unless you communicate them clearly, you can't expect anyone to anticipate what they are or realize they're going unmet. Sometimes we have to have those hard conversations in order to stay obedient to God's will for our lives.

I used to be a serial people pleaser. The thought that somebody could *possibly* be upset with me would consume my every thought until the situation was mended. I was perfect shark bait. If you want to swim with the sharks, you need to get really familiar with one word: *boundaries.* They're that important! You have to draw the line on toxic relationships in your life that are taking your time, your joy, and your resources. This means that you can't please everyone, and that's okay! I love this advice from author Cheryl Richardson:

"If you want to live an authentic, meaningful life, you need to master the art of disappointing and upsetting others ... living with the reality that some people just won't like you. It may not be easy, but it's essential if you want your life to reflect your deepest desires, values, and needs."

Of course, our goal is not to upset or disappoint anyone, but we have to come to terms with the fact that we can't make everyone happy all of the time. God never asked us to! Galatians 1:10 (NIV) says, *"Am I now trying to win the approval of human beings, or of God? Or am I trying to please people? If I were still trying to please people, I would not be a servant of Christ."*

If we try to perform for the approval of toxic friends, it will ultimately pull us away from God's will for our lives.

Gary and I discovered that if we were going to do business, ministry, and protect our time with our family, we had to set some firm boundaries on our time. Since we worked the weekends for church, we established Monday as our family day. Every staff member, whether on the church side or business side, knew our rule: no meetings, conferences, get-togethers, or seminars were allowed to be scheduled for us on Mondays. We also didn't check work emails or take work-related calls that day.

"What you allow is what will continue."

—Anonymous

When you set boundaries, you have to be prepared to fight for them. Gary and I had to take a stand for our Monday rule often. Sometimes we didn't want to! An important client would ask to meet on a Monday, and we'd have to explain our situation and ask to do a different day, risking the loss of the client. The incredible part was we never did lose a client over it! In fact, people respected that we put our family first and were more eager to do business with us. That's what boundaries do: they inspire people to respect you. They show that you respect your time, yourself, your family, your ideas—and that others should as well.

Set Yourself up for Success

One of the biggest factors to successfully dealing with sharks is taking good care of yourself! If you approach a shark when you're hungry, angry, lonely, or tired, you're going to be more susceptible to negativity, criticism, and manipulation. Make sure you are protecting the boundaries in your life, so you can operate out of a healthy place emotionally, spiritually, and physically.

The first quarter of 2017, Gary's and my schedules were packed with overseas conferences, speaking engagements, and nonstop travel. The one thing we forgot to schedule was REST, and at the end of that quarter, both of us were jet-lagged and exhausted. I realized we were on a fast track to burnout as leaders. Many friends in ministry had urged us to take a sabbatical, but for some reason or another, every year we cancelled, downsized, or scheduled over it.

The sad thing was we thought we were doing the right thing!

It can feel like giving, giving, giving is the best thing you can do for the people around you, but unless you're also taking the time to receive, you can actually end up hurting yourself and them more in the long run!

"Life is a marathon, not a sprint; pace yourself accordingly."

—Andy Burfoot

Gary and I finally took a month long sabbatical, and that time of rest and listening to God was one of the greatest choices we've ever made. That month break enabled us to help people in a much greater way than we ever could have before when we were trudging along exhausted. God's plan for you is to give from a place of wholeness, not from burnout.

If you need a break, don't feel guilty about taking it! You can only put your needs on hold for so long before it starts to affect your emotional, mental, and even physical well-being. Today, if you feel overworked, stressed, or depressed, put some downtime on your calendar to spend time with God and your spouse. Don't accept guilt from others who don't understand your life or schedule and its demands, because someone may just say, "It must be nice!" Simply respond to their guilt-dipped dart with a smile, and say, "God is good." He is, and He values you, so don't hesitate to place the same value on your life and time.

Even Jesus, who was perfect, took the time to get away and talk to God. So why would we be any different?

I know it can feel like giving a priority to your needs is selfish, but remember, life is a marathon, not a sprint. It's important to stop and ensure you're practicing the kind of self-care that is going to keep you on your God-given assignment for years to come. And when the people in your life ask you for the same favor, then you will be in a place of wholeness to show them the same support!

Remember Who the Real Enemy Is

Ephesians 6:12 (NIV) says, *"For our struggle is not against flesh and blood, but against the rulers, against the authorities, against the powers of this dark world and against the spiritual forces of evil in the heavenly realms."*

What somebody did to us may have been wrong, but we have to remember that we aren't dealing with flesh and blood. God loves that person and has a purpose for their life. We have all been a shark at a certain time or in a certain situation in our lives! Forgive others in the same way you would want people to forgive you. Forgiveness isn't just how you treat someone, it's how you choose to SEE someone. As we deal with sharks, it's so important that we keep the right perspective about who they are, so we don't let bitterness take a hold in our hearts.

"Every time I judge someone else, I reveal an unhealed part of myself."

—Anonymous

Forgiveness isn't a feeling; it's a choice that requires corresponding action. When our children were small, they'd often get into squabbles about toys or head-butting matches of "he said, she said." I'd listen to what each of them had to say and try to determine the source of the problem. Once I figured it out, I'd require the offending child (or children) to apologize for what they had done or said.

Boy, it could be a process to get them to admit their wrong actions and resolve the conflict.

On the other side of the equation, we taught the child who had been offended to say, "I forgive you," when they received the apology. Then, we expected them to hug each other. Whether or not they could hug was telling. If they couldn't hug each other, we knew there was still a problem—someone was holding back. And it made it easy to tell which child was either not truly sorry or had not forgiven and released the offense to God.

Jesus told us to pray, *"And forgive us our sins, as we have forgiven those who sin against us"* (Matthew 6:12, NLT). Then in verse 13, He goes on to say, *"And don't let us yield to temptation."*

Yes, they're related—forgiveness and temptation.

Because if you don't truly forgive others, you will be led into temptation—to retaliate against them and take action into your own hands! And that action will be sinful, guaranteed—anger, bitterness, division, slander, and maybe even physical or financial retribution.

Sound familiar?

Many people are serving prison sentences today because of the hurt and fury they unleashed when they didn't forgive and they gave in to the temptation as a result. If you knew a road was going to take you off of a cliff, you wouldn't stay on it, right?

You'd take a detour. You'd change directions. You'd set a new course.

Forgiveness is the detour that keeps you from taking the same road to regret over and over again. It gives you the ability to let go of yesterday and get on the right path. Forgiveness is a choice. The Word of God paints a picture of who you are, what you have, and what you can do. And the Word of God calls you out of regret, fear, worry, and unresolved hurts. You still have to make the choice each and every single day to walk it out, but it will get easier as you program your heart and renew your mind to God's Word.

God's nature is to forgive. Human nature is to get even.

All too often, when we get hurt, we see ourselves as victims. We feel upset, confused, angry, discouraged, and maybe even depressed or suicidal. We go through extremes of sulking or thinking of how we can pay the offender back—hurt them like they hurt us. We picture the person and rehearse what they did to us and how we can get even. And if we're upset with ourselves, we may try to get even by harming ourselves. That's the root of many addictions, cutting behaviors, and why people sabotage relationships with others or their own successes.

ACTION ITEMS

Is there a relationship where you are reaping what somebody else is sowing? What boundaries do you need to set to rectify this relationship?

_____
_____
_____

Is there a shark in your life that you've held unforgiveness toward? Complete the following exercise:

Picture yourself standing face-to-face with the person who wounded you, rejected you, stole from you, or hurt you.

Now, picture what you'd like to do to get even.

What would you tell them? Would you like to physically harm them?

Now, just as you are ready to yell at them, slap them, shoot them, reject them, cut them down with your words, or whatever it is you want to do…

Imagine Jesus stepping in front of you, standing between you and the person who has caused you so much pain. Looking into your eyes, He says compassionately to you, "*Whatever you want to do to them, do to Me instead. Unleash your hurt on Me. I paid for their sins, their offenses, and their mistakes, just as I paid for yours. What do you want to do to Me to get even with them for their offenses against you?*"

Ouch, right?

Because you're not going to inflict pain or nasty words on Jesus, are you?

So then He says, "*Forgive them as I have forgiven you. Turn them over to Me. Trust Me with this pain and hurt. Only I can be trusted to justify and judge. No man or woman has the ability to make either decision. On the scales of justice, all men and women are guilty. My sacrifice is sufficient for you both.*"

My friend, drop your weapons.

Release your pain and say, "Father, forgive them. I forgive them." When we choose to forgive, we're set free from the prison that others' sinful actions were intended to build around our hearts.

CHAPTER TWELVE:
DON'T BE A SHARK

"When you throw dirt at people, you're not doing a thing but losing ground."

—Zig Ziglar

Every time a shark attacks us, we have the choice to forgive and keep moving toward our destiny or to become a shark ourselves. And trust me, you may find yourself tempted at times when dealing with difficult people!

Don't let a wound from a shark turn *you* into a shark. It's so much more rewarding to follow God and be obedient to Him than it is to get even. We've had people attack our reputation, our family, our finances, and the list goes on, but God always vindicates us.

"*The Lord will fight for you while you keep silent*" (Exodus 14:14, NASB). If you're tempted to take up an offense and fight back, give it over to God!

When we started to build our business, we faced pressures we couldn't overcome on our own. It was in that pressure cooker of bills being behind, commission sales, and struggles that some of the first sharks appeared in our married life.

Personality wise, Gary has always been the steady-plodding installer, and I've been the salesgirl. That's how we actually met each other! While students at Oral Roberts University, he took a part-time job installing mini-blinds and woven woods. I answered an ad he had posted for his employer, a Spirit-filled Catholic lady named Pat, who hired me on the spot to sell what Gary would install. That's what I love about Gary—his word is his word. We are both hard workers and givers.

I had stayed up all night preparing for our sales meeting the next morning. The morning of our sales meeting, 15 insurance agents settled into our office extension. It was a small but adequate office ad-joined to our home with its own entrance. After working most of the night on sales campaigns, slogans, our newsletter, and contest rules, we were excited to start the new year growing our financial services business. Gary began sharing our business strategy with the team, but it didn't take very long into the meeting for one of the district managers to stand up and address my husband. "You couldn't make anyone successful," he stated sharply. Another district manager stood up and said, "Yeah, I agree." Gary stumbled through his words and managed to hold his composure together to finish the meeting. What started as a great anticipation of forward motion seemed to abruptly hit the wall. Later, Gary shared with me that he literally pinched his leg during the meeting to keep from losing it and just walking out. That night, laying in our bed feeling defeated, we cried, our dreams crushed under a weight of low esteem. Voices from the past haunted us both. "Stop your dreaming. Someday, you'll grow up!"

In our naivety, we thought if we gave in to these managers' demands for several years and worked hard to make them successful, they would be loyal. They would do their parts. We had given up so much of our profits to help them. We rented a high-rise office, thinking that would make the difference for them. We even advanced them monies they hadn't yet earned. There were times my husband drove to the bank to make their deposits and cover their debts. Eventually, they went their own ways to pursue whatever was the next big thing. We repeated doing this through the years with various people who came and went in our sales organization. The names changed, but too often the same attitudes would surface in managers.

However, we stayed with our plan. We kept working and believing and growing in ability. One day, 10 years after the meeting disaster, our business was acknowledged as the number one office in the nation. Strangely, a call came from one of those meeting "sharks." "Congratulations! I see you're the number one office in the nation!" "How did you know that?" my husband asked this man, a blast from the past. It was the other guy who stood up in the meeting that had called to tell him! That night, my husband said, "When God says He will prepare a table for you in the presence of your enemies, He's not joking."

Both guys were still in the same place financially and maintained the same attitude they had 10 years earlier. What if we would have quit because we believed they were right?

Often, the weapon we are most tempted to fight back with when somebody hurts us is our words. We may want to say something to their face, or worse yet, go behind their back and slander them.

We must choose to get better, not bitter!

Back in that meeting, Gary literally pinched himself to keep from lashing back at those sharks. When a shark attacks, guard your mouth! Your words have power! Proverbs 15:4 (NIV) tells us, *"The soothing tongue is a tree of life, but a perverse tongue crushes the spirit."*

We have all heard the saying, "Sticks and stones may break my bones, but words will never hurt me," but just because a word can't draw blood doesn't mean it can't do some serious damage. In our media obsessed culture, words are spoken so quickly and so reactively, without any pause or reflection as to what the consequences will be, but words have incredible power.

Your mouth is a dynamic weapon.

The Holy Spirit wants to use your mouth to heal the sick, prophesy, cast down the enemy's strongholds, and more, but the enemy wants to pervert your speech because he knows your words are a powerful weapon for God's Kingdom.

Be mindful. Be on guard. Be aware of the words that are coming out of your mouth.

Psalm 141:3 (NIV) tells us *"Set a guard over my mouth, Lord; keep watch over the door of my lips."*

If you had to put $20 in a jar every time you spoke a negative word about the situation you're going through, would you be poor by the end of the month?

Think about this…

When you open your mouth to speak, God will speak through you, if you let Him! You are His ambassador, His representative. You represent God to everyone you meet—including sharks!

Let's take a look at Ephesians 4:29 (TPT): *"And never let ugly or hate-*

ful words come from your mouth, but instead let your words become beautiful gifts that encourage others; do this by speaking words of grace to help them."

There are going to be people in situations in life that look innocent but turn out to be sharks. And on the other side, sometimes the people you thought were rough around the edges turn out to be loyal people. I'm sure you've heard the saying, "Don't judge a book by its cover." Only God knows somebody's heart and intentions; let Him be the judge. Give it over to God, and He will vindicate you!

There may be times when God asks us to do something that doesn't make sense to us, but since we know His heart is for us, we can confidently step out in obedience. God sees the bigger picture—He knows the beginning from the end. We may only see a small part of the equation, but God's Spirit directs us around obstacles we aren't even aware of. Deuteronomy 31:8 tells us God has already gone ahead of us and made a way for us. All we have to do is trust Him and listen for His voice! That's why it is so important that we seek the Lord and find out what God is saying to us about situations, relationships, and people. When you're tempted to speak badly about someone, give it over to God. Don't become a shark.

Letting Go of Offenses

Have you ever held onto something longer than you knew you should? Maybe it was a toxic relationship, a disappointment, a mistake, a negative thought, or even words somebody spoke over you…

Letting go can be hard!

"God, grant me the serenity to accept the things I cannot change, the courage to change the things I can, and the wisdom to know the difference."

—Reinhold Niebuhr

Wow. *"The serenity to accept the things I cannot change."*

How often do we waste our mental and emotional energy on things we can't change? We worry about the future, regret the past, feel insecure about ourselves, and hold onto painful decisions other people have made.

...but what would happen if we just let it all go?

Luke 12:25-26 (NIV) say, *"Who of you by worrying can add a single hour to your life? Since you cannot do this very little thing, why do you worry about the rest?"*

Our anxious thoughts accomplish nothing! In fact, they can paralyze us from moving forward. They can make us feel discouraged, victimized, alone, unworthy, angry, depressed, insecure, untrusting, and fearful. We may think the emotional baggage and toxic thoughts we allow ourselves to carry will protect us from getting hurt again, but they don't. They only keep us from embracing the freedom and blessing God has for us right now.

"Life will only change when you become more committed to your dreams than you are to your comfort zone."

—Billy Cox

So how do you know when to let go? And once you're ready to let go, how do you actually do it?

To identify whether it's time to let go of something in your life, start by asking yourself:

- *Is it based in LOVE or in FEAR?*

- *Does it line up with the Word of God?*

- *Does it apply to the present?*

- *Is there anything I can do to change it?*

- *Is it going to hold me back from obeying God?*

- *Has it already held me back?*

- *Is it affecting my emotional well-being?*

- *Is worrying about it going to make a difference?*

Things we need to let go of come in all forms and fashions. They can be thoughts, people, situations, hurts, sin, and fears. If you've identified an offense, shark, or sharklike quality in yourself that you need to release to God, here are three places to start:

1. Pray.

"Any concern too small to be turned into a prayer is too small to be made into a burden."

—Corrie Ten Boom

Ask God for the strength and wisdom to proceed. Give it to Him! Letting go of things that are holding you back is an exciting process because it will free you to live the life you want to live, but it will also require emotional growth to get you there.

God will give you the peace and grace to make the hard decisions!

2. Get a new vision.

"The only thing worse than being blind is having sight but no vision."

—**Helen Keller**

Start renewing your mind to what God says about your situation and focusing on what He says is true, not on what past experiences have trained you to believe. If you are dealing with a fearful or harmful mind-set, this is especially crucial. It's hard to let go of the past and embrace the future when we're living in fear.

"A man without a vision for his future always returns to his past."

—**Anonymous**

Start thinking God thoughts and discover the confidence to let go of the things that aren't meant for you!

3. Make a change.

"Only I can change my life. No one can do it for me."

—**Carol Burnett**

If you're dealing with a toxic situation in your life, you may need to make a physical change moving forward. Sometimes the best way to ensure we won't return to the negative situation in our lives is to draw a clear line in the sand. It may require separating yourself from the situation or having an honest conversation with a difficult person.

When we hold on to emotional disappointments, offense, heartbreak, and bitterness toward others, we only end up hurting ourselves! In order to move on, identify the actions you need to take to let go once and for all. When we let go of the things that aren't God's best for us, we find something so much better!

"Bitterness is like drinking poison and waiting for the other person to die."

—Joanna Weaver

In order to regain our joy, we have to give our hurts to God and allow Him to heal us—spirit, soul, and body. Hebrews 12:1 (NIV) says, *"Therefore, since we are surrounded by such a great cloud of witnesses, let us throw off everything that hinders and the sin that so easily entangles. And let us run with perseverance the race marked out for us."*

ACTION ITEMS

Have you ever let hurt or fear inspire you to act like a shark to somebody else? How did it make you feel?

_____

_____

_____

When we hold on to hurt, it hinders us from fulfilling our God-given destinies. Jesus wants you to be free from those tormenting emotions. He already paid the price for your emotional healing; all you have to do is receive it!

Pray this prayer today:

God, I give you my heartbreak, my disappointed expectations, and everything I have held against the people around me. I love you, and I cast my cares on you. Heal my heart and renew my joy. Amen!

CHAPTER THIRTEEN:
EMBRACING FREEDOM

After decades of marriage, raising a family, ministry, and business, I've learned a POWERFUL lesson...

How to be *HAPPY.*

You're probably thinking, *"That's crazy, Drenda! Everyone knows how to be happy!"*

Sure, I knew how to be happy when I got my way and life was going right... **but what about when everything was going terribly WRONG?**

What about when sharks were attacking me left and right? Or when I was living in an old farmhouse that had plants growing through the windows, I was digging through couch cushions to find enough money to get the kids McDonald's, and I found out bees had set up their home in the bedroom my sons shared?

Making the choice to rejoice and walking in freedom wasn't so easy on those days...

I remember going through the drive-through with my children one day, and I was stressed, tired, and worried about different circumstances with sharks in Gary's and my life. If you've ever gone through the drive-through with five little ones in your vehicle, you know the ordering process can be frustrating. I tried my best to order as each child loudly chimed in, in unison, with their order.

The McDonald's worker handed me our food, and I pulled away. The smell of french fries filled the car, and my worries started to fade as I grew more excited to eat. I drove down the road and pulled over where we could enjoy our meal in the car.

I handed each child a meal, but as I went to pull mine out, my hand reached the bottom of the bag.

They forgot my food!

Now I was stressed, tired, and HANGRY. Yes, that is a real emotion! I raised the cup of Sprite in my hand in a burst of anger; and as if on cue, the lid on the paper cup popped open, sending a small tidal wave of Sprite all over the car. My kids watched in silent awe, and I heard my oldest daughter, Amy, start to cry.

I looked up at the Sprite-stained roof of our van with the soundtrack of my daughter softly crying in the backseat. I had totally blown it…

We all have bad days, but you don't have to let your circumstances keep you from walking in the freedom you have in Christ. I learned how to make the choice to rejoice the hard way, but you don't have to!

"Be selective with your battles. Sometimes peace is better than being right."
—Anonymous

I realized that I needed to change my mind-set. It was time to shut down the pity party for one. I put a sign up in our bathroom that said, **"Make the choice to rejoice."** Every time I started to feel bad for myself, I went into the bathroom and read that sign.

Then I looked at myself in the mirror and gave myself a little pep talk. *"Drenda, this isn't your forever... You're going to bigger and better places! You can do it! You were made for this!"*

I regained my joy and took back my day!

The powerful lesson I learned was that my happiness was MY CHOICE. I could CHOOSE to have a good day—to be unaffected by screaming toddlers, a difficult person at work, or something somebody said that was intended to wound me.

It was an incredible discovery: I was the master of my emotions.

"Nobody can steal your joy unless YOU give them permission."

Every single day, we have two choices: we can simply react to everything happening around us, or we can take action and create the lives we want to live. If we put our happiness in other people's hands, we're going to be disappointed. Not only that, but we'll be on an emotional roller coaster.

Don't give someone else the keys to your happiness!

It's incredibly freeing when we take back the responsibility for how we feel. When we react to others' actions, it sets us up to be the victim. When we maintain the fact that we own our emotions, we free ourselves to be victorious in all circumstances!

Matthew 16:19 (NIV) says, *"I will give you the keys of the kingdom of heaven; whatever you bind on earth will be bound in heaven, and whatever you loose on earth will be loosed in heaven."*

The keys are in your hands. What are you going to do with them?

Freedom from Insecurity

"You wouldn't worry so much about what others think of you if you realized how seldom they do."
—Eleanor Roosevelt

Insecurity.

It's the silent voice that tries to tell us what to do, what to think, and how to feel about ourselves and the people we love. Insecurity is the wave that we ride into the jaws of sharks. Unchecked, it becomes a PRISON around us… It often makes us more susceptible to shark wounds, keeps us paralyzed in unhealthy situations, and worse yet, makes us want to get out of the water for good.

Insecurities can haunt us!

- *Do people think I'm weird?*
- *Am I lovable?*
- *Am I capable?*
- *Do I need to lose weight?*
- *Have I made too many mistakes?*
- *Can I really do this?*
- *Am I pretty enough?*
- *Am I a failure?*

Tormenting thoughts begin to swell in our minds, and we can become paralyzed in the water beneath the pressure. Our perception of reality can actually be changed by these thoughts!

When I was a young woman, I struggled with perfectionism; occasionally I still do. I wanted to be perfect—hair, clothing, shoes, makeup. I didn't realize at the time that my insecurity was derailing my God-given purpose. My worth was wrapped up in other people's opinions. If I was perfect, I thought people would accept me, people would love me. It wasn't true. People can't give you what you don't have and they can't give you what they don't have.

When you don't know who you are in Christ, you feel insecure, but when your identity is firm in Christ, you are free to be who you are, who God made you to be.

When you learn who you are, you trade perfectionism for enthusiasm—enthusiasm for relationships, for life, for your God-designed dreams, and, most importantly, for joy and laughter!

When we tolerate insecurities, we start bouncing our identities off of the people and media around us, looking for something to confirm or deny our inner fears…

Did anyone compliment my outfit today? Am I as pretty as that movie star? Did she say she was busy because she didn't want to hang out with me?

We become shark bait!

And the worst part is Satan will put people, media, and situations in our lives to discourage us and feed those insecurities.

"The reason why we struggle with insecurity is because we compare our behind-the-scenes with everyone else's highlight reel."

—**Steven Furtick**

 Insecurities can cause us to:

- Endure hurtful or unhealthy relationships

- Lash out at the people around us

- Use manipulation to get attention and affirmation

- Become easily offended and overreact to situations

- Battle depression, fear, and hopelessness

- Withdraw from the people we love

- Beat ourselves up over small mistakes

- Give up on ourselves

- Become possessive of the people we love

"If you set out to be liked, you would be prepared to compromise on anything at any time, and you would achieve nothing."

—**Margaret Thatcher**

My friend, insecurities will either make you shark bait or a shark!

In the early years of our marriage, my insecurities caused me to doubt Gary's love for me. I kept waiting for him to hurt me like the men in my past had, because deep down, I didn't feel lovable.

I was always waiting for the catch…

One night, I locked myself in our bathroom, crying.

"Drenda, I don't know what to do," Gary said from the other side of the door. I could hear the desperation in his voice as he began to cry. "I just can't get through to you! When are you going to realize that I'm not those men that hurt you? I love you, and I'm not going to leave."

I had been hurt by sharks in the past, and instead of walking in the freedom Jesus paid for from those wounds and allowing Him to heal my hurt, I was still walking around with those bleeding cuts. It took those words to finally break down the wall of insecurity I was hiding behind.

Before that night, I never realized that I had been FILTERING Gary's words and actions through shark attacks in my past!

If we tolerate insecurity, it's like a weed that chokes out our hope, happiness, and trust in the people around us.

When we water insecurity, it grows!

When Insecurity Knocks

So what do you do when insecurity comes knocking at your door?

How do you shut down the seeds of self-doubt before they blossom into paralyzing uncertainty?

Philippians 4:6-7 (NIV) say, "*Do not be anxious about anything, but in every situation, by prayer and petition, with thanksgiving, present your requests to God. And the peace of God, which transcends all understanding, will guard your hearts and your minds in Christ Jesus.*"

So first, as I mentioned earlier in this chapter, we're instructed to PRAY. If we feel insecurity beginning to grab ahold of us, we need to turn to God and ask Him for His help in the situation. We need to pray for the grace to walk in confidence.

Philippians 4:8 goes on to say, "*Finally, brothers and sisters, whatever is true, whatever is noble, whatever is right, whatever is pure, whatever is lovely, whatever is admirable—if anything is excellent or praiseworthy—think about such things.*"

The second thing we're called to do is to change what we're LOOKING at!

If you are battling an insecurity, you need to adamantly shut down the voices and images speaking that into your life. If you feel bad about your body or looks, stop spending hours browsing through photos of Instagram models and movie stars in tabloid magazines. Start putting your focus on things that are going to encourage you instead!

Did you know that God put everything in you that you need for your destiny? With Him, you are lacking nothing, and are able to do impossible things!

"No one is you, and that is your power."

—Anonymous

When negative thoughts start to rise up in you, challenge them with the Word of God.

Psalm 139:14 (NIV) says, "*I praise you because I am fearfully and wonderfully made; your works are wonderful, I know that full well.*"

People may have hurt you in the past, disappointed you, or broken your heart. Jesus didn't come just so He could pay the price for our physical healing. He also paid the price so we could have emotional freedom, confidence, and devotion to Him! Psalm 34:18 promises us that God is near to the brokenhearted and He saves those who are crushed in spirit.

So how do we receive healing?

First, we have to deal with ourselves. Our natural minds want to *see*, but we know faith is the evidence of things *not* seen. We have to have confidence that the Word of God has the power to bring to pass what it says. When we have confidence in what the Word says, we enact a spiritual law that brings it into existence! Mark 11:24 (NIV) says, "*Therefore I tell you, whatever you ask for in prayer, believe that you have received it, **and it will be yours**.*"

God's love for you is perfect, and He sees the potential He's put in you. God created you to live a life of freedom from the shark attacks in your past and to walk out your true potential! You were created with a purpose. You were FEARFULLY and WONDERFULLY made. God made you, and He doesn't make mistakes!

ACTION ITEMS:

Have insecurities ever held you back or made you shark bait? If so, what insecurities?

_____

_____

_____

Read Psalm 139:14. What does this verse mean to you?

_____

_____

_____

Look up 2 Corinthians 3:17. Where does it say we find freedom?

_____

_____

_____

CHAPTER FOURTEEN:
WHY YOU'RE UNDER ATTACK

It was the morning of evangelist Billy Graham's funeral when I was awakened in the wee hours before dawn to a stirring by the Holy Spirit. I was keenly aware that Gary and I must focus, laser focus, on what God had called us to do to take the message of the Kingdom to America and the nations. It was a gentle stirring but nonetheless would not let me sleep. I felt volumes downloaded to me in a few hours, words I would speak to my husband as he began to wake a few hours later. Gary shared with me that while flying in the night before, he also had been stirred. The words "purpose, passion, and pursuit" were rolling around in his spirit. The realness of the Holy Spirit's drawing spoke to us both that just as a woman has labor pains before the birth, we had been in such a season for a few years, and now was the time to strategically plan with our team and children to seize our Kingdom ministry with focused clarion strategy.

In my morning wake-up call, I saw clearly that my husband and I had supported many people and many ministries through the years, and God was dealing with us to not back up or shy away from our calling. Although the church had grown to 3,000 and our media ministry was impactful, we were never completely comfortable sharing our vision and asking for others to help us engage that vision. I knew very clearly that God was gently rebuking us to believe in what He had called us to do enough that we would be willing to give voices to our own work and believe that others had been called to help us just as we had spent the last 30 years helping others do their work.

Gary and I have always been more comfortable supporting and giving than asking or receiving. Many times, we both would confuse accepting others' help for us with our desire to help others. Consequently, we were usually on the giving end of every relationship, to our joy, but this alone would not propel the mission God kept telling my husband we had been given. God made it clear to us, as we talked, that we could not function without the other side of this relationship—giving *and* receiving—and just as we had been faithful, others also wanted to faithfully help us now, but we wouldn't "ask for help" in the form of openly sharing our vision.

Later, watching Billy Graham's funeral via livestream, I realized the body of Christ was also being stirred by the death and legacy of this great leader to stand and step into the climactic final scene of the ages, to prepare for the return of Christ. For three weeks of turmoil in our ministry prior to this, I kept flipping open to Scriptures about leadership and building.

One story was about Nehemiah and how he was moved to rebuild the walls of Jerusalem. Nehemiah had wept when he heard about the devastation of Jerusalem and the broken walls of the once great city. He secured a release from his employer, King Xerxes, to go, with a blessing, to rebuild Jerusalem's walls.

It's not just important to have a heart for the vision and confirmation. It's just as important in the execution of the vision to share it with others who can come alongside you to share in the vision. As God instructed us, we were not sharing the vision for various reasons, but none of them were good. Nehemiah traveled to Jerusalem and shared the vision with the Israelite people. *"I also told them about the gracious hand of my God on me and what the king had said to me. They replied, 'Let us start rebuilding.' So they began this good work"* (Nehemiah 2:18, NIV).

As Nehemiah did this, contenders and accusers appeared during the work to stop him and his team. Nehemiah, now challenged, had to fight both the enemies of his efforts *and* rebuild the walls. Winston Churchill fought the overwhelming voice of his own party that demanded he surrender Britain to Hitler, and in the midst of this great opposition, developed a plan to call upon his own people to surrender their boating vessels to remove the trapped British forces from destruction. Nehemiah's plan succeeded, and so did Churchill's, but not without a fight. "I know the plans I have for you," says the Lord, "to bless you, not to harm you, and to bring you to a good end." God has a good end to any endeavor He has asked of you, but to be sure, anything worth doing will be met with some opposition. Surrendering is not an option we can afford. Too much is at stake! Opposition is not the proof you've missed God, but almost always is the guarantee you're onto something that hits His mark.

"For such a time you have been called into the Kingdom" is a phrase we have heard very much, but are we engaging this calling? Be sure if God is calling, Satan is countering. But greater is He that is in you than He that is in the world. It's imperative that we don't let sharks stop the rebuilding and advancing of God's work in the earth. Whatever parts you or I have to play in that calling, we are all called to do our parts if Jesus is our Lord. Every man, woman, and child has some part to play in the Kingdom, and now is that time. It's important we have laser focus on "advancing the Kingdom of God that revolutionizes lives."

Who or what will you allow to waylay you or cause you to stop fighting the good fight of faith? It's a good fight because it is the fight between good and evil, a fight of the ages to either obey God and His way or to let evil have its way with the lives of people.

Nehemiah succeeded with the rebuilding of the wall by utilizing important principles that we need to examine to deal with difficult people. The tactics of shark warfare are evident in his story. I recognize these tactics that have been used against us, too, schemes that in past days caused us to be reticent to confidently share our calling and ask others to join us to build. Maybe these tactics are working to stop you from your destiny at this very moment. The attack against God's plan on Nehemiah's life (and on each of us) took these forms:

1.   Ridicule and mockery

2.   False accusations

3.   Distractions

4.   Discouragement

The enemies of Nehemiah mocked him and made fun of his mission. The goal of mockery is to intimidate us into thinking thoughts like these: "How foolish of me to believe that this could actually happen for me!" "Maybe I missed God!" "I don't have what it takes to succeed at this!" The ultimate goal of all of these strategies is to get you to quit! Make no mistake, if you don't understand what's going on with these strategies, you may actually surrender to the enemy when victory is so close.

PEOPLE WILL MAKE FUN OF WHAT THEY DO NOT UNDERSTAND BECAUSE THEY DIDN'T HEAR THE DIRECTION THEMSELVES.

When Nehemiah kept on task with His work, knowing He had the support of King Xerxes and, most importantly, the King of all, they moved in with a new tactic. They falsely accused Nehemiah of rebelling against the king. Interestingly, they accused Nehemiah after what was in their own hearts! They were the rebels and troublemakers.

 ## PEOPLE OFTEN ACCUSE YOU OF WHAT IS IN THEIR OWN HEARTS.

I've often seen this where money is concerned and especially when ministries grow into larger, more successful endeavors. The sharks will gather to ridicule ministries, and when that tactic doesn't stop the work, false accusations of a leader's motives or mishandling of money are waged toward the leader. And if one leader fails, be sure misguided news agencies and people will beat that drum until the perception is that every ministry leader is guilty of the same. Sharks smell blood and move in for the kill. However, they choose to bury stories that show the incredible good works of ministries.

How long will we fall for their accusations and stop building ministry in the earth? There is never an issue of lack in God's Kingdom. There is plenty of money in the earth. There are plenty of resources in the earth. It's tied to harvest, both the harvest of souls and the finances needed in order to reach them. Both are needed, and if either one is missing, ministry ceases. Jealousy and competition for territory or funding can even motivate those inside the church to attack one another. Ministries are not competing with one another but, rather, competing against the enemy of the souls of men, Satan. He is our real competition! If we reach people and bring them into God's vision for their lives, they will resource His work. We just have the wrong perception of Kingdom finances, a perception that is propagated mostly by those who want to stop the work. Unfortunately though, about every decade, a smear campaign happens to decapitalize the body of Christ from accomplishing its mission.

Philippians 2:15 (NASB) says, "*So that you will <u>prove yourselves to be</u> <u>blameless and innocent</u>, children of God above reproach in the <u>midst of</u> <u>a crooked and perverse generation,</u> among whom you appear as lights in the world.*"

Believers get fearful when they hear accusations and cease to support churches and outreaches financially. The enemy knows this and has succeeded in part with this tactic. Then the defunding sets ministries back from advancement since all endeavors require capital! And with the Internet and social media, it's easier than ever for anti-God forces to wage war against Christian business endeavors and ministries with slander campaigns. We have personally had groups who declare freedom from religion as their goal threaten to destroy us financially as we build God's Kingdom. They have threatened our family as well. Shall we stop rebuilding? No! The apostles said, "Lord, behold their threatenings and grant that your servants may speak boldly, with signs and wonders accompanying us."

Answering a Bully

How do we handle those who threaten or accuse us? Believers and leaders must stay with their work and deflect the sharks just as Nehemiah did. When challenged by sharks, Nehemiah 2:20 (NIV) says, "*The God of heaven will give us success. We his servants will start rebuilding, but as for you (sharks) you have no share in Jerusalem or any claim or historic right to it*" (my name-calling emphasis added). Our trust must be firmly planted in the purpose God gave us: to continue to answer the heavenly vision to build, to take territory, to possess all His promises in our work and lives, and to fight for a heavenly cause! Nehemiah and the people also prayed and believed God would both protect and help them resist their enemies.

Continue to declare the vision, and stay with the work. Only those who pose a threat to the enemy get that kind of attention, so count yourself in good company: "so persecuted they the prophets." Jesus assured us that if some hated Him, some will hate you as well. You are not a hater just because someone hates what you stand for if you are standing for God's Word. Remember, they accuse you after what is in their own heart. Trust in God in the midst of accusations, and even though it may feel like you are being slowed in your progress, the stamina you build through their resistance against you will form muscle that makes you stronger and more resilient in the long run. Not only will you rebuild the walls in your life, but also you'll have the capacity to maintain them because of the process that happens while you build and fight for your vision. This requires trust and discipline. Each challenge is an opportunity to personally grow more valuable and trained for greater works of service. Little by little, character and discipline form the unshakable foundation of our lives and faith. Accept discipline as a friend that will reward you in the end, both here and in the hereafter. God's Word will produce what it promises if we are only patient to stay with the work.

We've all heard talk is cheap. Let's keep building while others are talking. If there's anything bullies do, they talk a good game. They sound threatening with their many words, but the best vengeance is to succeed at doing what God has called you to do. Billy Graham outlived all of his enemies, and his legacy gave him greatness here and in the life to come. Was he a perfect man? I think not. There are no perfect men or women, only Jesus. But because he put his trust in Jesus, God perfected his life to build the Kingdom. Build a business for God with God. Build a family. Build a legacy. Build a wall that protects your life and family from evil by obeying God wholeheartedly regardless of what others choose.

Be a Dolphin!

Dolphins have been known to actually encircle a person to protect them from a shark attack. And the dolphins themselves have waged a group counterattack against sharks. They hit the shark head-on, ramming them with their noses until they have defeated and destroyed the shark. But they can only accomplish this by staying unified as a team. There is power in unity and protecting one another. The dolphin recognizes this is life or death, and we must do likewise as the body of Christ! Even when someone on the team falters, if they truly turn from their error and get back in the race, we need to encircle them and fight off the sharks. Interestingly, Nehemiah invoked this strategy, and we see in Nehemiah 3:1-32 a complete list of all the different men and their families who built sections of the wall next to their houses, each doing their parts while working side by side. Unifying around the work, whether it was building a business, a city, or a nation, the people worked together, each doing their part and staying with their purpose with passion while ignoring the accusers, detractors, and discouragers.

 PEOPLE DISTRACT THROUGH DEMANDS AND UN-REASONABLE INQUIRY.

As a business or ministry leader, people who want attention and mean harm will demand meetings with you or explanations of why you are doing what you have heard from on high to accomplish. Reasonable people want the understanding and acceptance they would offer to others. It's normal to want to explain yourself or help someone understand your reason. However, you can't reason with a shark! They're out for blood, not reason. You can't reason with evil. Evil has as its goal to steal, kill, and destroy. Giving it an audience is an invitation. Nehemiah's enemies demanded he come and talk to them about what he was doing and explain himself to them. If he would have been distracted into taking the opportunity to leave his work to answer their arguments, he would have acknowledged their right to question him, thus empowering their inquisition. Instead, he refused by saying, "Why should I leave this good work to answer you?" He answered their demand with a wise question that left *them* in the place of inquiry. Instead of getting on the witness stand and being cross-examined, he tactfully turned the inquiry around by calling their motive into question with a question. It is a mistake to spend your time in the midst of those who will wear you out with their ill-concocted questionings. Remember, you cannot reason with evil. These men had no desire to understand Nehemiah's vision or to share in the work. They were decoys meant to draw him into deeper water, their territory, to move in on him.

In our church's earliest days, there was a troublesome man with serious control issues in his life. His family was deeply troubled because of him, and his children had rebelled against his legalistic control. We wanted to help them for the kids' sakes. Even though he found consistent fault with our ministry over distorted issues he rigidly held, he didn't leave the church! He stayed to be a shark and make trouble. I had to watch my attitude because his belligerent criticism made me inwardly angry, but outwardly I tried to be polite. After a Sunday church service as we shook hands with people leaving, he took my hand as if to shake it but wouldn't let go. As I tried to pull back my hand, he squeezed it firmer. He stared me in the eye and, with a penetrating glare, said, "You will call my wife tomorrow, and you will tell her she is (he used some expletive names), and if she doesn't do what I say, she's going to hell." At first a chill hit me, then anger rose up. I wanted to stomp his foot, but I managed to get out of his grasp and said, "I will do no such thing." And I turned from him to shake hands with others. (It wasn't long before I stopped shaking hands with everyone!)

This man called our home phone that week and started the same conversation (if you could call it a conversation). He refused to let me off of the phone. You might say, "How can someone make you stay on the phone?" I would say, "I'm finished with this conversation. I'm hanging up now," but he would keep talking. Now, I'm a southern girl, and we say good-bye and the other person says, "Good-bye." He wasn't saying, "Good-bye" and kept talking to keep me on. I didn't want to be rude; I was trying to be polite. I was getting angry on the inside again. After a little more of his nonsense, I realized I couldn't reason with this person. He doesn't have common courtesy. After three or four times of stating "I am getting off NOW," I finally said, "At the count of three, I'm hanging up." I counted and hung up. Fair warning. You can't be polite with the devil either!

One Sunday a while later, he walked in with a check and gave it directly to my husband (my husband had given him some terrific financial advice that paid off), so I thought, *"Praise God, he's coming to his senses, and our long-suffering has finally helped change him!"* The man showed up Monday to see Gary and said, "I gave that check to the church only if you face the church east toward Jerusalem and stop saying this and do what I want and…. My husband reached into the desk drawer and pulled out his rather large check and tore it in half and handed it to him. Our church was small and we could have used the money, but the manipulation wasn't worth any price! I later asked my husband, "Why didn't you put that check in with the ministry deposit this morning?" Gary said, "I knew that check had strings attached and he would show up to pull them, so I was ready!" I laughed. Eventually, the guy moved on after his wife left him. I always hurt for his family, but the enemy used my heart for his family to manipulate and hurt me for several years. You cannot take false responsibility for everyone's problems and the risk of stealing your time, energy, and calling for a person who will not make right choices. You can care more than they do! There is a time to draw the line and hang up on a toxic relationship. Let it go!

As you start to see progress in your endeavor, be wise not to mistake the beginning for the end. Success can be a distraction to the work as well. Beware of the temptation to leave the mission not only at the invitation of an enemy but also at the beckoning of a flatterer as well. There are those who have impure motives and want to exploit you for their gain. They may seem like they are for your work, but their real motive is that your work and effort will transfer into gain for them. It's one thing to deal with an obvious enemy, but sometimes it's subtle and hard to see the motives of those you may even call friends. So are we to trust no one? Of course not! But stay true to what God said regardless of friend or foe, and make sure you don't compromise the vision whether you receive an inquiry or a pat on the back.

There's obviously a time to share vision and answer questions, especially with those who are working alongside the vision with a right heart, but to answer critics who have no skin in the game and only desire to take you off the wall is a trap. Stay the course and finish the work. Don't stop except to rest and reward yourself along the way. Don't relinquish. It's not finished until it's finished. And there is no finish until you and I cross the finish line and can say, "I've completely run my course. I finished my race. There's a victor's crown laid up in store for me!"

HOW TO RECOGNIZE A SHARK

1 They always have issues with any authorities they can't manipulate. (Romans 13:1-4)

2 They are critical and faultfinders. (Titus 3:9)

3 They prey on the innocent. (Hebrews 13:5-6)

4 It's about them, not Jesus. (Acts 24:15)

5 They are gossips and talebearers. (Psalms 94:4)

6 They hang out with others that do the same. (Psalms 141:4)

ACTION ITEMS

1. In Psalm 27:1 (KJV), it says, "*The Lord is my light and my salvation; whom shall I fear? The Lord is the strength of my life; of whom shall I be afraid?*" Who do you tend to be afraid of or intimidated by? Why?

_____

_____

_____

2. How does God's promise to be with us help us face sharks and situations?

_____

_____

_____

3. In what area will you be bolder and how?

_____

_____

_____

CHAPTER FIFTEEN:
SHARK PROOF

It's time.

It's time to jump in the water and boldly pursue God's assignment for your life.

It's time to fearlessly swim with the sharks.

It's time to confront the situations and people problems holding you back!

It's time to set boundaries around what is important!

God created you for something special. He created you to make a difference. Don't give up on God's plan just because you're afraid, uncertain, or because you face obstacles or difficult people. You have to put your belief in what God says about you—that you *CAN* do it!

As you look at God, at His Word, and at what He says about you, you'll discover your identity in *Him* instead of in your performance or in your *lack* of performance; you'll discover that you are loved, accepted, and forgiven. Then, you'll be empowered by grace to do things not through your own strength but through Him and His strength!

Whenever I feel like I can't handle a situation, or I can't do something, I tell myself, "Sure I can." I can do ANYTHING I need to do through Christ who strengthens me (Philippians 4:13). YOU can do anything you need to do through Christ who strengthens you too!

Jesus has already purchased the victory for you on the Cross. It's up to you to know the truth, to live the truth, and to enforce it when you're in the battles. Your life isn't about what you can accomplish on your own, but it is about what you can accomplish with God. When you walk with God, your life can be better than you ever imagined!

Over the years, I have learned that when I let go of my control over situations and choose to submit to God's will, I feel at peace. The battle is the Lord's, but you must walk it out!

Seeing changes as new beginnings, rather than endings, makes you open to all the wonderful opportunities that God puts in front of you.

God loves you and wants to help you win in ALL the areas of life. I assure you, nothing is too big or too small for His time and attention. I want to encourage you to go to God before you become anxious or fearful. As you jump headfirst into the water, remember:

Face Your Fears

God is bigger than your circumstances and bigger than ANY of the obstacles standing in your way! John 14:27 (NIV) tells us, "*Peace I leave with you; my peace I give you. I do not give to you as the world gives. Do not let your hearts be troubled and do not be afraid."*

Believe me, if God has brought you to it, He will bring you through it. He will protect you and give you the victory!

The enemy has so many tactics to scare you out of your God-given purpose. Don't let fear take root. Instead, take up the Word of God, the sword of the Spirit, and use it to extinguish fear, insecurity, and doubt.

Psalm 119:28 (NIV) tells us, *"My soul is weary with sorrow; strengthen me according to your word."* The Word of God is your strength; use it, speak it out loud, and put it before your eyes every day.

Trust God for the Outcome

When unexpected news comes your way, do you get sweaty palms, knots in your stomach, or have trouble sleeping?

You're not alone! For years, I was that woman: fearing that things wouldn't turn out well, trying to control the things that were far beyond my control. If you usually respond to change that way, remember, our God is the God of new beginnings!

Second Corinthians 5:17 (NKJV) tells us, *"Therefore, if anyone is in Christ, he is a new creation; old things have passed away; behold, all things have become new."*

Part of staying joyful in times of change is trusting that God has called you out of the darkness, made you a new person, and given you a new life—one of peace, joy, and provision.

Give what's beyond your control to God. He is before you and ahead of you, and He will orchestrate the victory in His perfect timing!

In 2 Corinthians 12, Paul speaks of a "thorn in the flesh" sent to torment him. This is the equivalent of what we would call a "pain in the neck" (sounds like a shark to me). This was a messenger of Satan sent to torment him so he would stop his powerful ministry and revelation. He asked the Lord to take it away from him, but God said, "*My grace is sufficient for you, for my power is made perfect in weakness.*" Paul further says, "*I delight in weaknesses, in insults, in persecutions, in difficulties, for when I am weak I am strong.*" We know from this passage that Paul's messenger was a group of sharks, the Judaizers who insisted that grace was not enough but that the law, including circumcision, must be followed. In other passages, we find they followed Paul around to persecute and insult him. Paul wanted it to stop! Yet God told him that HIS GRACE (His power and ability) in the situation was enough! Paul could rejoice that even though he felt troubled by these accusers, he was even stronger because God empowered him where he was weak. God's grace could do what Paul by himself could not!

May I encourage you with the same words! You may not be able to stop people who are trying to hinder your progress, but you have God's grace to walk above the insults and trouble with victory, and His grace is enough for you! If you will press on toward the mark, you will win, regardless of opposition. You will overcome and triumph in Christ Jesus. You will outlive your persecutors. God will deal with your enemies. Greater is He that is in you than he that is in the world!

Leap for joy when you are attacked by sharks for the Kingdom's sake! The joy of the Lord will strengthen you by grace! You will deflect their assaults and swim valiantly toward your destiny!

Celebrate New Opportunities

No matter how big or scary the change, if you walk through it with a positive attitude, you can have peace. I believe sometimes God moves us into new situations because we are too afraid or anxious to do it ourselves.

Don't listen to what the world tells you is impossible; we know with God ALL things are possible! If you take your focus off of your fears and potential problems and focus on your hopes for the future, God will continue to reveal His amazing purpose for your life.

God never stops giving us BIG dreams; sometimes we just stop hearing them, often because of sharks! I want to empower you to open your heart to what God is trying to tell you. His love will help you rise far above your fears, doubts, and insecurities and into the extraordinary future He has for you.

I hope this book has inspired you and given you the encouragement and wisdom you need to walk into the future with hope and courage.

It's time to partner with God and BOLDLY pursue your dreams, because through Him you are SHARK PROOF!

"Listen carefully: I have given you authority [that you now possess] to tread on serpents and scorpions, and [the ability to exercise authority] over all the power of the enemy (Satan); and nothing will [in any way] harm you"

(Luke 10:19, AMP).